Arbeitsblätter

J. D. Salinger
„The Catcher in the Rye“

17 Arbeitsblätter
mit didaktisch-methodischen Kommentaren

Sekundarstufe II

von Traudl und Wiklef Hoops

Ernst Klett Verlag
Stuttgart Düsseldorf Leipzig

Die Seitenverweise dieses Heftes beziehen sich auf folgende Textausgabe:
J. D. Salinger, The Catcher in the Rye. Penguin Books/Ernst Klett Verlag Stuttgart.
Klett-Nr. 3-12-573806-7

Parallel zur Textausgabe des Romans ist erschienen:
J. D. Salinger, The Catcher in the Rye – Annotations and Study Aids.
Klett-Nr. 3-12-573808-3

Gedruckt auf Papier aus
chlorfrei gebleichtem Zellstoff,
säurefrei.

Die Deutsche Bibliothek – CIP-Einheitsaufnahme
Ein Titeldatensatz für diese Publikation ist bei Der Deutschen Bibliothek erhältlich.

1. Auflage 2000 A

Internetadresse: http://www.klett-verlag.de
E-Mail: klett-kundenservice@klett-mail.de
Stadtplan S. 22: Jürgen Neumann, Rimpar
Illustrationen S. 24, 29, 36: Christian Dekelver, Weinstadt
Umschlaggestaltung: BSS Werbeagentur Sachse und Partner, Bietigheim
Druck und Bindung: Wilhelm Röck, Weinsberg. Printed in Germany.
ISBN 3-12-927823-0

Introduction

Contents

This workbook consists of 17 worksheets and additional material on Jerome D. Salinger's *The Catcher in the Rye* together with teaching notes, which contain hints for teaching and interpretation and answers to the tasks. It is intended for grades 11–13 of grammar school ("Grundkurse" and "Leistungskurse").

The worksheets offer many opportunities for students to engage in active and cooperative learning. The tasks are varied and contain many suggestions for working in pairs or groups. There are also a few tasks which require creative writing and acting.

The structure of the novel
Apart from a few longer flashbacks this novel is structured chronologically. The first and third part are narrated in the traditional way, the second part represents a collection of picaresque episodes, which are mainly held together by the hero's continually deteriorating physical and spiritual condition and the three central themes "communication", "sexuality", and "phoniness".

Reading the novel
There are as many good arguments for reading a novel through at one go as there are for a step by step approach. Considering the rather loose structure of the novel, a step by step approach does not seem to be advisable. On the other hand, it may be expecting too much of the students to read the novel in one go. Therefore, we have decided on reading the novel in three parts: Chapters 1–7, 8–20 and 21–26.

The novel is still a favourite with adolescents (cf. the respective websites) as it directly relates to their psychological and social situation. Therefore the motivation of the students should be no problem.

Due to Salinger's professed aversion to movies, there is no film version of this successful novel.

1. School

The novel we are going to read is about a boy of your age (Holden Caulfield) who has, among other things, problems with school. Write your own opinions of school into the first column of the following worksheet. After you have read chapters 1–7, you will be able to fill in the second column ("Holden's opinion").

Opinions of school

Aspects of school	Your opinion	Holden's opinion
school in general		
teachers		
school subjects in general		
favourite subjects		
evaluation of one's own performance		
schoolmates		

2. Different experiences with school

Compare the following two reports. Why did the girls like or dislike school?

Emma Slavsky (age 15)

High school is basically high school, and so this school was really not that different. I complain a lot about school, because school is not built for me. [laughs] I went to a magnet school[1] before, and the reason I liked it was because I had so many friends there. That's basically what makes or breaks it, I think, because high school is so horrible – it's just a bad place. And it's not meant for anything but being bad to teenagers. When I talk about high school it's not about my high school, it's about *all* high schools – my old school has the same problems, except it's very diverse.

In my new school they have this big facade of being very liberal. The school is supposed to be this incredibly diverse place, which is the biggest load of BS[2] I've ever heard in my *life*. Thirty percent minority, maybe thirty percent black, I don't know. The point is, there's all these kids that come here from Chicago – like me – except they're black… [sighs] They're taking kids and sticking them in regular classes – which are horrible – and not dealing with what they bring to school, and what they lack. They see them as a deficit; they see all of us as a deficit.

1 *magnet school* – USA, an academically demanding public school, especially in inner cities, that attracts students from a wide area

2 *BS* – (AE vulgar) bullshit, i.e. nonsense

Rebekah Evenson (age 19)

I went to a Montessori school that the parents developed. The parents, and the kids too, we built it with our hands. It was this one-room schoolhouse, in the shape of an octagon, made out of wood – a lot of salvaged lumber[1]. It was a *great* school – all different ages – and that's really how I got to where I am today, which is being a nineteen-year-old college grad. There were no grades or grade levels – so, when I was ready to read a book, I just read it; and when I was ready to do tenth grade math, it didn't matter that I was in fifth grade. There was no competition in terms of doing better than other people. Cheating wasn't something that you would even think about doing, because [laughs] you wouldn't get anywhere with it – there'd be no reward whatsoever. Your achievement wasn't measured in terms of anything but how you are doing, and how you can do versus how you are doing. It made school fun, it took the edge off learning. I didn't have any idea that school was supposed to be boring and you were supposed to hate it – until I went to public school in sixth grade.

From: Sydney Lewis, *"A totally alien life-form". Teenagers*, New York: The New Press, 1996, p. 344

1 *salvaged lumber* – wood for constructing houses, bridges, etc. which could still be saved from other constructions that had been destroyed or demolished

3. Truancy – a way of dealing with problems in school?

Children with problems in school often simply skip school.

Truancy is unexcused absences from school, without parental consent. Truant adolescents typically have a history of doing poorly in school. They see their classes as "stupid," their teachers as hostile, and would rather be anywhere *but* school. On days when they are absent, they usually spend their time hanging out with other alienated teenagers. They are more likely than other adolescents to get involved in delinquency and drugs. Psychologists used to believe that the truant's absence from school and negative attitudes toward school led to academic failure. They are now coming to believe that academic failure is often the cause, not the consequence, of truancy. These teenagers see school as a setting in which they repeatedly fail, and so develop antieducation attitudes and beliefs to protect their self-esteem.

From: L. Steinberg/A. Levine, *You and your adolescent. A parents guide for ages 10 to 20*, New York et al.: HarperCollins Publishers, 1990, p. 305

If you were the parent of a truant child, what would you do to help your child?

1. Reading the first seven chapters

Please read the first chapters of "The Catcher in the Rye". It is not necessary that you understand every word, with the exception of the chapter you are going to examine closely. The "Special dictionary" explains words you might have difficulties with. The "Vocabulary for discussion and essay writing" contains word fields and collocations you might find helpful for a discussion in class and essay writing.

Note down in the following table the main persons Holden meets or tells about in each chapter and select quotations (sentences or short expressions), which are either characteristic of Holden or the person(s) concerned:

Chapter	Person(s)	Characteristic quotation(s)
1		
2		
3		
4		
5		
6		
7		

Note down characteristic descriptions Holden gives of himself and his situation:

2. Holden in the Internet

If you have any questions you would like to discuss with other people outside your school, you can try the following URL (last checked 17.6.00):
http://hatteraslight.com/navy/JDSalingerhall/mobydick.html

al dictionary +++ Special dictionary +++ Special dictionary +++ Special dicti

a...

a the best mark in American schools
ad (coll.) short for advertisement
Andover town in Massachusetts with the famous Philipps Academy for boys (founded 1778)
to apply o.s. to sth. to give all one's energy and attention to
ass (taboo) the buttocks
Atlantic Monthly well-known literary and political magazine

b...

backasswards (taboo) with the ass backwards, in reverse order, wrong
bag (sl.) ugly girl, prostitute
bastard child whose parents were not married, (sl.) despicable man
Benedict Arnold (1741–1801) American Revolutionary general who became a traitor
Beowulf long Old English heroic epic in alliterative verse
to be up the creek (coll.) to be out of luck, to be in trouble
big shot (fam.) important or influential person
bitch female dog, (sl.) an ill-tempered woman, a woman with loose morals
booze (to) (coll.) alcoholic drink, to drink in excess
brace device for supporting a weak part of the body
break (sl.) a piece of good fortune
buck (sl.) US dollar
buddy (sl.) familiar form of address, (often to strangers)
bunk (sl.) nonsense
Burns, Robert Scottish poet (1759–1796)
butt (coll.) buttocks
buzz telephone call

c...

to caddy to carry the golf player's clubs
can (sl.) toilet, buttocks
check bill in a restaurant
checkers ‚Damespiel'
to chew the fat (coll.) to chat
to chew the rag (coll.) to gossip about trivial matters
to chisel (coll.) to cheat, to swindle
to chuck (coll.) to throw
cop (USA) policeman
corny (sl.) out of date, often heard or repeated
crack (sl.) joke, derogatory remark
crap (taboo) excreta, (sl.) nonsense, rubbish
credit points given for completing a course of study
crew-cut ‚Meckifrisur'
crumb-bum (sl.) worthless person, tramp
crumby (sl.) lousy repulsive
to cut out to stop doing
cute (coll.) clever, attractive

d...

David Copperfield famous autobiographical novel by Charles Dickens; its hero had an unhappy childhood but ends up as a successful author
dandy neat, smart, very good
D.-Day June 6, 1944, the day of the American invasion of Europe in World War II
diarrhoea ‚Durchfall'
to die (coll.) to be eager
dopy (sl.) as if doped, stupid, slow
dorm dormitory, room in which students sleep
dough (sl.) money
doughnut a ring-shaped cake of sweet dough, fried in fat

e...

Eustacia Vye passionate heroine of Thomas Hardy's novel "The Return of the Native"

f...

f lowest mark in American schools
faculty staff of a university or college
falsies stuffing in a bra to give women's breast a better or larger shape
Farewell to Arms novel by Ernest Hemingway
feel (taboo) the act of touching a girl intimately
to fiddle to make aimless movements
flit (sl.) male homosexual
to flop (sl.) to fail, to collapse
to flunk a subject to fail a subject
fuck you a taboo expression of decisive rejection

+++ Special dictionary +++ Special dictionary +++ Special dictionary +++ Spe

g…

gal (coll.) a young pleasant girl or woman
to get the axe (sl.) to be dismissed
to get to first base (sl.) to start to get intimate with a girl (from baseball)
to get pretty run down to become exhausted
to get wise to become aware of
to give the freeze to treat coldly
to give the time (sl.) to have sexual intercourse
glob drop or lump
goner hopeless case
gore (clotted) blood
grandstand the main seating structure for spectators
Great Gatsby, The famous novel by Francis Scott Fitzgerald (1896–1940)
grool imitates a strange pronunciation of the word 'girl'
guts bowels (‚Eingeweide')
gym (coll.) abbreviation for gymnasium = hall for gymnastics

h…

half-assed (taboo) inefficient
halitosis bad smelling breath
hall closet small room or cupboard for clothes
hard up in want of
to haul to pull forcibly
heck (coll.) 'hell'
to hit the road to start on a journey
hoodlumy-looking looking like a criminal
to horn in to intrude, to interfere
horny (low coll.) lusty
to horse around (sl.) to joke, to refuse to be serious
horse manure nonsense
hot shot important, successful person

i…

I. Q. intelligence quotient
Ivy League the term refers to certain outstanding American institutions of higher learning which, with one exception, were founded during the colonial period of American history. The most famous American universities such as Harvard, Yale, Princeton and Columbia belong to the Ivy League group.

j…

Jack used for an unknown person
to jiggle to rock or jerk lightly
to jitterbug to dance to jazz or swing music in the 1940s and early 1950s
job (coll.) almost any object, procedure, machine etc., esp. one of good quality, often with reference to a car
junk rubbish, silly talk

k…

to keep tab(s) on to have under observation
to kid to joke
king ‚Dame' im ‚Damespiel'
knockers (sl.) female breasts

l…

to lay a fart (vulg.) ‚furzen'
lick in jazz: a short phrase of improvisation
liquorice ‚Süßholz', ‚Lakritze'
Lord Randall an old ballad
lulu (sl.) anyone or anything of extraordinary size, appearance, force etc., used derisively as well as admiringly

m…

mitt baseball glove
morgue building in which bodies of persons found dead are exposed for identification
moron feeble-minded person, a fool

n…

to neck to kiss, to caress, to pet
nope (coll.) no
N.Y.U. New York University

o…

to ostracize to exclude from society, from a group

al dictionary +++ Special dictionary +++ Special dictionary +++ Special dicti

p...

panic (sl.) a person or thing considered extremely humorous or entertaining
pansy (coll.) effeminate youth, male homosexual
to pass out (sl.) to faint
Pencey Prep a prep(aratory) school is usually a private school which prepares students for college; being often expensive, they connote high social status, wealth and snobbery
Penn Station Pennsylvania Station in New York
physical a health examination
pig (sl.) a girl with sloppy appearance and/or morals; among students: any girl or woman
pimple ‚Pickel'
pimpy-looking looking like a man who finds customers for a prostitute
pitcher (motion) picture
to plug (sl.) to shoot
pole a bat (in baseball)
pro a professional
to puke (sl.) to vomit
to put it on (sl.) to exaggerate
putrid (coll.) very disagreeable

r...

racket excitement, gaiety, noise
rake an immoral man
regular pleasant, agreeable, conforming to accepted conventions
Return of the Native, The novel by Thomas Hardy (1840–1928)
Ring Lardner (1885–1933) American short story writer
to rip off to remove by tearing vigorously
rubbernecks (sl.) gaping sightseer, inquisitive person
to rush (sl.) to court a girl intensively

s...

screwball (sl.) mad, crazy person
to shoot the bull (sl.) to flatter, to gossip
to shoot the crap (taboo) to shoot the bull
to sign out for to enter one's return in a book or list
slob (sl.) a fat, average person
snot (vulgar) ‚Rotz'
sonuvabitch (taboo) son of a bitch (‚Hundesohn')
to squeal (sl.) to betray
stance posture, the way a person stands
Stekel, Wilhelm (1868–1940) psychotherapist who believed with Adler that the importance of the unconscious had been exaggerated. He utilized the concept of the life-line or life-style.
stiff (sl.) a corpse
to stink up (sl.) to spoil, to ruin
to straighten so. out (coll.) to tell the truth
swell (coll.) wonderful, excellent
to swipe (sl.) to steal by snatching

t...

tail (taboo) a girl or woman considered only sexually
tap dance ‚Stepptanz'
tee in golf: small piece of wood, rubber, etc. on which the ball is placed before being struck
throw the unit by which something is sold
turtleneck ‚Rollkragen'
to take a leak (sl.) to pass urine (‚urinieren')

w...

wad a roll of notes, money
wheeny-whiney cf. 'to whine' = to complain in a childish way
whosis any person whose name is unknown or forgotten
a witch's teat cf. 'teat' = nipple of the breast
wizard (coll.) a person with outstanding gifts
wutchamacallit what-you-may-call-it

y...

Year Book contains school events, names and pictures of students for a school year
yella streak tending to be cowardly
yellow (coll.) cowardly

Vocabulary for discussion and essay writing

1. Growing Up
– children, teenagers, adolescents, adults
– go/pass through a (physical, emotional and intellectual) crisis; the difficult/critical period/phase of adolescence/puberty
– be at the stage when ...
– be afraid of growing up/change; long for peace/stability/permanence
– learn to cope/come to terms with one's (own) sexuality; form a relationship with a girl; establish relations with the opposite sex
– take over/accept responsibility for one's own life/other people;
decide on/choose a career

2. Emotions
– feel alone/lonely/lonesome/sad/miserable/depressed/desperate/rejected;
be often/frequently depressed; suffer often/frequently from depression;
have frequent bouts/attacks of depression
– be nervous/embarrassed/afraid of/frightened of *(not formal)* scared of
– have ambivalent/mixed feelings about; find something boring/repulsive/disgusting, be repelled/disgusted by; hate
– be indifferent to/interested in/concerned about; care/worry about

3 a) Communication: General
– chat with somebody about; talk to/with somebody about; have a chat/talk with somebody about
– be looking for/in need/search of a friend/friendship/(somebody's) understanding/love/
a personal relation-ship with/someone to talk to/company
– fall into conversation with somebody about/strike up/start (up)/have a conversation with somebody about; be in/get/come in(to)make/establish contact with
– send/take/give/pass on a message to ...
– refuse to talk to/with somebody; attempts at communication fail/never come to anything/are not successful/break down/collapse

3 b) Communication: Telephone
– dial a/somebody's number; phone/ring/call somebody (up): *(not formal)* give somebody a ring/*(slang)* a buzz; make a (quick/short/brief) phone call to;
talk to somebody on the phone
– (tele)phone booth *(AmE)*/box *(BE)*/*(formal)* kiosk
– answer the phone; hang up (on somebody); ring off *(BE)*

4. Love and Sex
– fall/be in love with; be fond of/affectionate towards
– date somebody; have a date with; go out with
– pat somebody (on); stroke somebody; kiss; neck/have sex/sexual intercourse with; seduce
– be sexually (in)experienced; be always talking about/preoccupied with sex;
boast of one's conquests
– see/regard/treat a girl as a(n) (sex) object/person in her own right/partner/individual/whole person/human being
– propose to; reject a proposal; marry; be/get married to
– prostitute; pimp; homosexual

5. Religion
– be a(n) Catholic/atheist; believe in; go to church/mass
– join a monastery; monk; nun
– minister; give a sermon, pray to …
– God; angels; Jesus (Christ); disciple
– carry crucifixes; sing Christmas carols
– collect money for charity; make a contribution (to a collection)

6. Death
– die of leuk(a)emia; commit/drive somebody to suicide
– go to/attend a funeral; bury (in a cemetery); visit a cemetery/grave; put flowers on a grave/tomb

7. Society: Adjustment and Rebellion
– accept/conform to/adjust to/make one's adjustment to/reject/rebel against the demands/norms/values of (a materialistic/middle class) society
– be disgusted/repelled by the indifference/insensitivity/phoniness/dishonesty/insincerity of the adult world
– run away/flee/escape/withdraw from the monotony/inhumanity of city life/urban society; run off/away to the woods to live the simple life

8. Education
– be at/go to/attend a(n) boys'/all-boy/single-sex school
– schoolmate/class(-)mate/room(-)mate
– share a room with, *(AmE)* room with
– be good at; take/pass/fail (in) an exam(ination)/a subject; *(informal esp. AmE)* flunk; failure
– expel somebody from school; *(informal)* kick somebody out; *(informal)* give somebody/get the axe (*AmE usually* ax); expulsion
– work harder at school/apply oneself

9. Health
– get/have (got)/suffer from TB/pneumonia/diarrhoea
– feel well/run(-)down/exhausted/dizzy/sick/better; faint; pass out; be sick; vomit / *(slang)* puke; have/recover from/get over a (nervous) breakdown
– make an appointment with/see/consult a psychoanalyst/psychiatrist; be treated in an mental/psychiatric hospital/psychiatric clinic/rest home/sanatorium *(AmE also)* sanitorium/sanatarium

10. Conflicts
– quarrel/fall out/have a(n) disagreement/argument (with somebody about/over); insult; apologize (to); accept an apology
– hit/punch*(informal)* sock somebody (in the stomach/on the jaw); shoot some-body
(in the stomach);
– smack somebody; knock somebody down/out

11. Language
– use teenage/colloquial/jerky/vulgar/obscene/crude language; slang; swear/four letter/taboo words; words imprecise/vague in meaning; generalizations; exaggerations
– have a poor/limited/restricted vocabulary; repeat favourite expressions/phrases; finish one's sentences with/add empty phrases; generalize; exaggerate; be inarticulate/unable to organize one's thoughts; digress (from the subject)
– tell the truth/lies
– erase/rub out graffiti/obscenities

1. The opening of "David Copperfield"

Holden is narrator and "hero" of "The Catcher in the Rye". He does not want to write like David Copperfield, the hero of the fictional autobiography "The Personal History of David Copperfield" (1849/50) by Charles Dickens (1812–1870), one of the most famous English novelists.

THE

PERSONAL HISTORY AND EXPERIENCE

OF

DAVID COPPERFIELD THE YOUNGER.

CHAPTER I.

I AM BORN.

WHETHER I shall turn out to be the hero of my own life, or whether that station will be held by anybody else, these pages must show. To begin my life with the beginning of my life, I record that I was born (as I have been informed and believe) on a Friday, at twelve o'clock at night. It was remarked that the clock began to strike, and I began to cry, simultaneously.

In consideration of the day and hour of my birth, it was declared by the nurse, and by some sage women in the neighbourhood who had taken a lively interest in me several months before there was any possibility of our becoming personally acquainted, first, that I was destined to be unlucky in life; and secondly, that I was privileged to see ghosts and spirits; both these gifts inevitably attaching, as they believed, to all unlucky infants of either gender, born towards the small hours on a Friday night.

I need say nothing here on the first head, because nothing can show better than my history whether that prediction was verified or falsified by the result. On the second branch of the question, I will only remark, that unless I ran through that part of my inheritance while I was still a baby, I have not come into it yet. But I do not at all complain of having been kept out of this property; and if anybody else should be in the present enjoyment of it, he is heartily welcome to keep it.

2. Comparison between Holden and David as narrators

Compare the opening of "David Copperfield" with the opening of "The Catcher in the Rye" and fill in your findings in the table on the next page. Also try to draw conclusions from your findings about the two fictive autobiographers.

	Holden Caulfield	David Copperfield
Situation of narrator		
Intentions		
How far into the past		
Emotional state of narrator		
Language and narrative technique		
Relationship to reader		
General characterization of the two narrators		

Which are the main qualities attributed to Dickens in the following text?

▶ **Charles Dickens**

b. Feb. 7, 1812, Portsmouth, Hampshire, Engl.
d. June 9, 1870 Gad's Hill, near Chatham, Kent
in full CHARLES JOHN HUFFAM DICKENS, English novelist, generally considered the greatest of the Victorian era. His many volumes include such works as *A Christmas Carol, David Copperfield, Bleak House, A Tale of Two Cities, Great Expectations,* and *Our Mutual Friend.*

Dickens enjoyed a wider popularity than had any previous author during his lifetime. Much in his work could appeal to simple and sophisticated, to the poor and to the Queen, and technological developments as well as the qualities of his work enabled his fame to spread worldwide very quickly. His long career saw fluctuations in the reception and sales of individual novels, but none of them was negligible or uncharacteristic or disregarded, and, though he is now admired for aspects and phases of his work that were given less weight by his contemporaries, his popularity has never ceased and his present critical standing is higher than ever before. The most abundantly comic of English authors, he was much more than a great entertainer. The range, compassion, and intelligence of his apprehension of his society and its shortcomings enriched his novels and made him both one of the great forces in 19th-century literature and an influential spokesman of the conscience of his age.

"Dickens, Charles" *Encyclopaedia Britannica Online*
<http://www.eb.co.uk:180/bol/topic?eu=114623&sctn=1>
[Accessed March 25, 1999]

Charles Dickens

1. Prep Schools

Preparatory Schools are, usually rather expensive, private schools which prepare for college. Below you will find an example of a contemporary prep school. What values are stressed in the advertisement? Compare this school with Pencey Prep and Elkton Hills as seen by Holden. Write an advertisement for Pencey Prep.

Tuition Fee 1998–99

Upper School	
If paid in full by July 10	$8550
If paid in two installments	$8800
If paid monthly (12 months)	$9100
Middle School	
If paid in full by July 10	$7920
If paid in two installments	$8175
If paid monthly (12 months)	$8480

THINK

where a rigorous grounding in skills and knowledge is just the beginning – where teachers and students share inquiry, reflection and analysis on the path to personal understanding

CREATE

where people celebrate the imagination in geometric proofs and formal essays, on canvas, computer and stage, in poetry readings and morning assemblies

BE YOURSELF

where people respect differences and can find their place in a diverse community

ASPIRE TO EXCELLENCE

where students develop winning attitudes in academics, athletics and arts

AND GO BEYOND

where beautiful surroundings, museums, concert halls and community service become classrooms that foster deeper understandings of one's self, others and the world

More than just a college preparatory school ...

A preparation for life with a higher purpose than self

2. Holden on school

Complete the table by filling in the second column ("Holden's opinion"). Compare your evaluation of school with that of Holden.

Opinion of school

Aspects of school	Your opinion	Holden's opinion
school in general		
teachers		
school subjects in general		
favourite subjects		
evaluation of one's own performance		
schoolmates		

3. Discussion about school

Discuss the pros and cons of schooling. Refer to your own experiences. What can be done about Holden? Write a dialogue between Holden and his mother after she has learned that he has been thrown out again.

1. Holden meeting other people

Act Holden's meeting with Mr Spencer, Ackley or Stradlater. Before acting write down key words on cards so that you don't lose your train of thought. Discuss the performance(s) in class.

2. Holden on other people

Holden makes quite explicit statements about other people. Give a condensed report on Holden's opinion of Mr Spencer, Ackley, Stradlater, his brother Allie, and Jane Gallagher. Use the following two worksheets.

How do you judge these people? Would you agree with Holden? What can be inferred from Holden's opinion about other people with respect to his own character and his likes and dislikes?

How does Holden judge other people?

Mr Spencer	**Ackley**	**Stradlater**
Your judgement:	Your judgement:	Your judgement:

Brother Allie	**Jane Gallagher**
Your judgement:	Your judgement:

3. Other people on Holden

Imagine, the psychiatrist in the hospital where Holden is at the time of writing his autobiography has the idea of finding out more about his patient by interviewing people who had regular contact with Holden at Pencey Prep (Mr Spencer, Ackley, Stradlater). How might they have described Holden? Enter your results into the following worksheet.

Write a short report in which the psychiatrist summarizes the essence of his interviews.

How do other people judge Holden?

Mr Spencer	Ackley	Stradlater

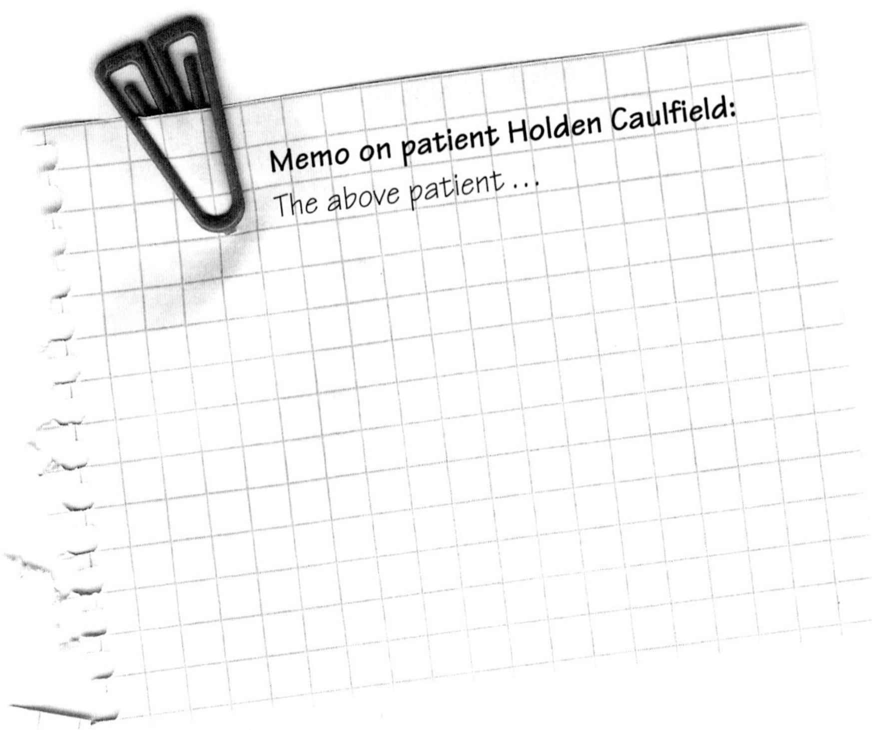

1. Holden's situation and character

On the spur of the moment, Holden decides to leave Pencey Prep three days before the end of term. Explain Holden's sudden decision by referring to his character and his present situation. Use the following worksheet to structure your observations.

Holden's situation and character

School	
Everyday life	
Last day	
Social	
Emotional	
Self-evaluation	
Opinions of others	
Dislikes	
Values ("likes")	

Write a letter to a friend and try to describe Holden.

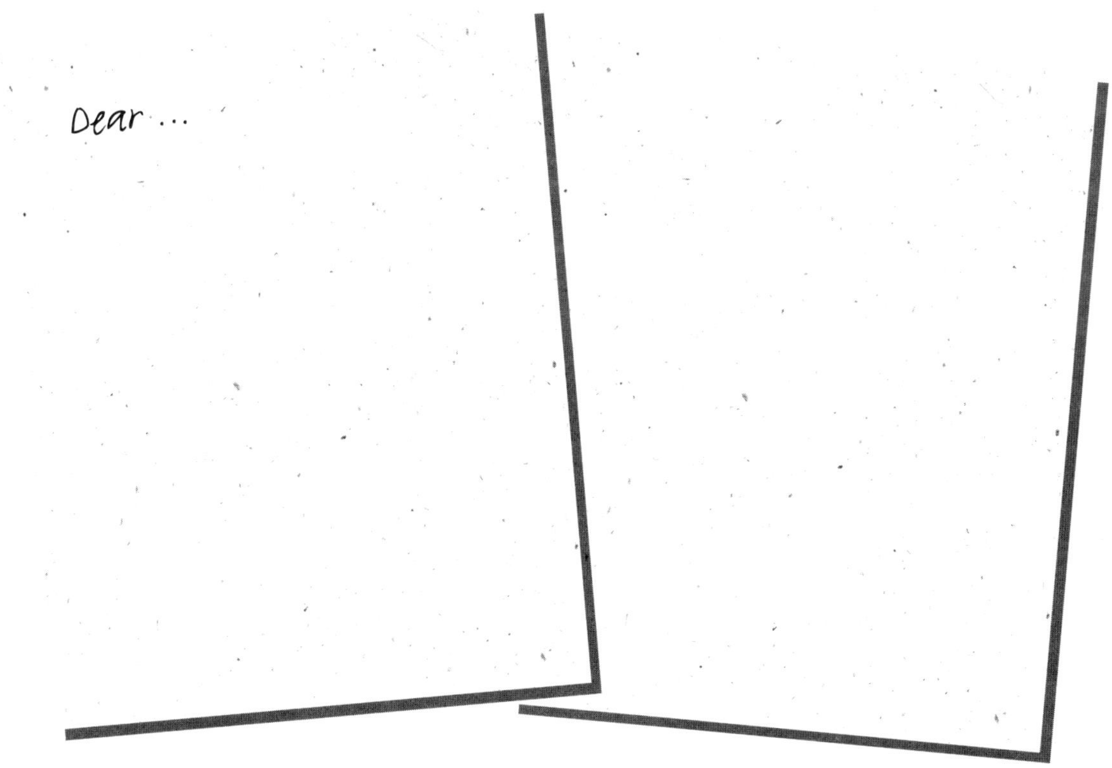

2. Holden – a typical adolescent?

Social psychologists divide the human life-span into several periods, starting with childhood followed by adolescence. Read the following article on "adolescence" and write the main "symptoms" of adolescence as depicted in this text into the diagram below. Is Holden a typical adolescent?

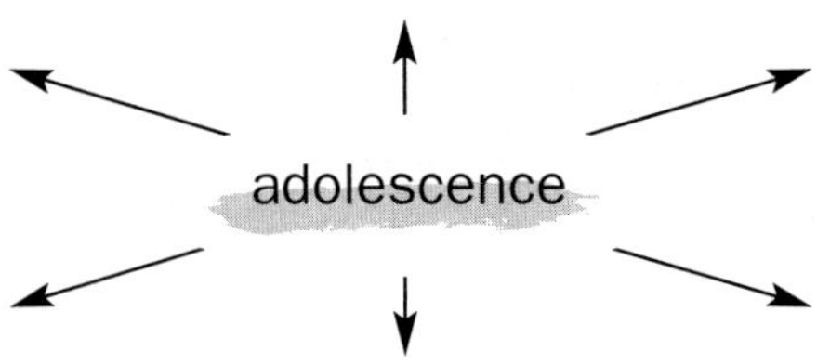

▶ **adolescence,** usually defined as the period of transition between childhood and adulthood. Although some writers equate adolescence with puberty and the cycle of physical changes culminating in reproductive maturity, adolescence is more commonly defined in psychological and social terms as beginning with pubescence and terminating vaguely with "adulthood." The term is a convenient label for a period in the life of an individual (approximately ages 12 to 20); such usage need make no commitment regarding the character of adolescent development or the specific nature of its causes (e.g., pubescence). [...]

Any period of life tends to be characterized by a group of developmental problems that are biological, psychological, and social in origin and timing. Among those that typically but not necessarily occur during the second decade of life are adjustments in the areas of heterosexual relations, occupational orientation, the development of a mature set of values and responsible self-direction, and the breaking of close emotional ties to parents. In a sense, such developmental tasks define adolescence and represent areas in which satisfactory adjustments must be made if future psychological development is to be possible.

Authorities are not in agreement as to the nature of adolescence. To the popular mind and to many specialists, adolescence is presumed to be a psychologically stressful and critical period, characterized by a variety of special types of behaviour.

According to one viewpoint, essentially biological and stemming mainly from psychoanalytic literature, adolescence is initiated at pubescence by the sudden upsurge of sex feelings following a sexually tranquil period of latency. Adolescence is the period during which the individual learns to control and direct his sex urges; it ends when such control and direction are established. The whole process is presumed to be highly stressful emotionally and to give rise to a variety of behaviours, ranging from avoidance of the opposite sex to the writing of diaries, which are thought to be characteristic of adolescence and which serve to reduce the sex-generated anxiety. A biological view of adolescence implies a certain universality of occurrence.

Cultural views also assume adolescence to be a stressful period, but one that occurs only under certain circumstances. Because children generally are not given graded opportunities for maturing experiences compatible with their physical and intellectual development, they experience a sudden widening of their world during their teens. This encountering of new ideas, concepts, values and types of people, and the sudden responsibility for self-determination and self-sufficiency, force an array of adjustments upon the comparatively inexperienced young person and generate much apprehensiveness and anxiety. Furthermore, the teenager has no defined role of his own in society but is caught in the ambiguous overlap between the reasonably clearly defined roles of childhood and adulthood. Sometimes treated as a child, sometimes expected to be adult, he is uncertain how to behave. Also, society serves to frustrate important psychological needs of the young person (e.g., sex and desire for independence), thus generating aggression or other reactions, many of a socially disapproved type. In all the various cultural views, adolescence exists in the degree that such conditions prevail in a particular culture or a particular home.

From: The New Encyclopaedia Britannica, vol. I, 15th ed. 1985, p. 104

3. "Being in the middle"

Compare Lucy's statement to Holden's situation.

Lucy Anderson (age 16)

It's weird being a teenager: you can't do things with the adults, because they do things that you have to be over eighteen to do; or they do things that you wouldn't understand; or things they think you wouldn't be interested in. When you deal with adults you're not really respected as much as an adult would be. But then you don't want to play with the little kids. You're only really accepted by other teenagers, you know? So you gotta kinda have your own little world – and that's why it's weird being a teenager.

When you're sixteen, you get freedom, or special privileges – you can get a job, and maybe that could be your escape. Or when you get your license, it's like, *"Yes!"* Me and my friends, we just find *any* reason to go driving. We won't have any particular place to go usually; we'll just drive, and talk, listen to the radio, waste a lot of gas … [laughs] But it's fun. We're escaping from being in the middle, I guess – from not really having anything else to do. It's kinda like our thing, our privilege. What's accepted, or expected: what we *should* do. I just got my license. My mom doesn't have a car, actually – she doesn't drive. But it's neat having it. It gives me a goal too: I can save up for a car.

From: Sydney Lewis, *"A totally alien life-form". Teenagers*, New York: The New Press, 1996, pp. 307–308

4. Holden's short "holiday" in New York

Imagine you were in Holden's situation. What would you plan to do in New York? Write your ideas into the following diagram.

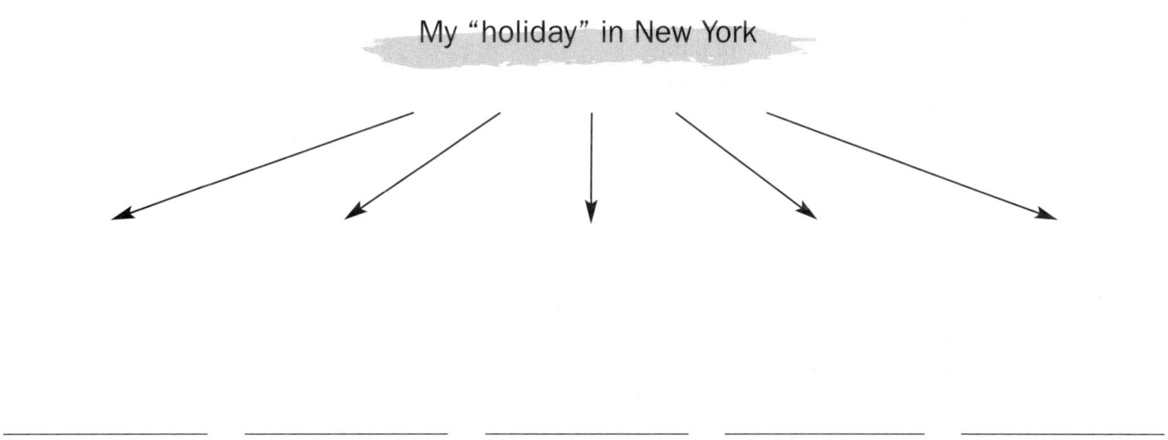

Photodisc

The skyline of New York – what do you associate with it?
Would you like to be in New York for a few days quite on your own?

Which of the numbered areas and buildings in the following map of New York do you know about?

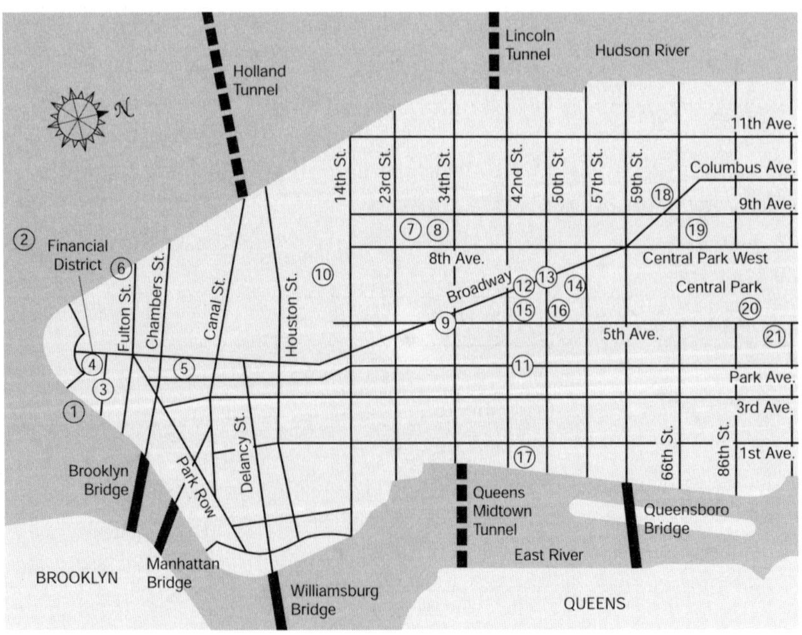

NEW YORK CITY

1. Staten Island Ferry
2. Statue of Liberty
3. Wall Street
4. New York Stock Exchange
5. Chinatown
6. World Trade Center
7. Madison Square Garden
8. Pennsylvania Station
9. Empire State Building
10. Greenwich Village
11. Grand Central Station
12. Times Square
13. Theatre District
14. Carnegie Hall
15. Rockefeller Center
16. Museum of Modern Art
17. United Nations
18. Lincoln Center for The Performing Arts
19. Museum of Natural History
20. Metropolitan Museum of Art
21. Guggenheim Museum

Please read chapters 8–20. Filling in the following worksheet will help you to keep track of the many characters and episodes depicted in these chapters. Don't try for completeness.

	Places	People	Themes/Topics/Problems	Page(s)
Saturday				
1.				
2.				
Sunday				
1.				
2.				

1. What could the two pictures symbolize?

2. Aims of communication

Why do we communicate with other people? Collect as many ideas as possible and try to categorize them afterwards.

3. Holden on his arrival in New York

When Holden arrives in New York, he immediately goes into a telephone booth "feeling like giving somebody a buzz". After 20 minutes he leaves it without having phoned anybody. Shortly afterwards he phones Faith Cavendish. Explain his behaviour and its result.

4. Holden in conversation

Here you find a selection of statements or questions of Holden in conversation. Find out who is being spoken to, try to recall each situation, and describe it. What do these quotes tell us about Holden?

1. "You give me a royal pain in the ass, if you want to know the truth."

2. "Did you ask her if she still keeps all her kings in the back row?"

3. "By any chance, do you happen to know where they go, the ducks, when it gets all frozen over?"

4. "You're a real friendly bastard."

5. "Allow me to introduce myself. My name is Jim Steele."

6. "This room stinks … I can smell your socks from way over here."

7. "How's your sex life?"

8. "Would you care for a cocktail?"

5. Analysis of "Holden-dialogues"

Analyze in groups the dialogues between Holden and Ackley (pp. 41–45), Sally (pp. 117–121) and Old Luce (pp. 129–134).

Dialogue between Holden and Ackley, Sally and Old Luce

Holden's attitude to partner	
Holden's aim(s)/purpose	
Holden's behaviour during conversation	
Reactions of Holden's partner	
Result	

6. Holden could have done better!

Write a dialogue between Holden and (Ackley, Sally, or Old Luce) which is more rewarding for both partners.

1. Love and relationship

Do you like this picture? What do you associate with it?

Bilderberg Hamburg

2. Holden's relationship with Jane Gallagher

Characterize Holden's relationship with Jane Gallagher and explain his reactions to Stradlater's dating Jane (pp. 26–29, 36–39, 69–73). Why doesn't Holden give "old Jane a buzz" (pp. 56+95) or says "hello" to her (p. 28)?

3. A meeting that never took place

Imagine, Holden is meeting Jane two days after her date with Stradlater. Write a dialogue between the two. How could the meeting end?

4. Holden on sex

Analyze Holden's attitude to sex by referring to his observations in the Edmont Hotel (pp. 55–56) and his meeting with Sally Hayes (p. 95, pp. 112–113). The following quotations might give you some help.

"I don't *like* the idea. It stinks if you analyze it." (p. 56) | "Sometimes I can think of *very* crumby stuff … it might be quite a lot of fun …" (p. 56)

"I keep making up these sex rules …, | and then I break them right away" (p. 56)

"She was really a moron. | But what a dancer." (p. 64)

"That's the thing about girls. Every time they do something pretty, even if they're not much to look at, or even if they're sort of stupid … | you fall half in love with them, and then you never know *where* the hell you are." (p. 65)

"It was a very corny book … | but I couldn't get that violin stuff out of my mind anyway." (p. 84)

"Sexy was about the *last* thing I was feeling." (p. 86) | "I was starting to feel pretty sexy …" (p. 83)

"I didn't even *like* her much, … | and yet all of a sudden I felt like I was in love with her and wanted to marry her." (p. 112)

5. Sex and brains

How would Holden's following statement apply to himself:

"I mean most girls are so dumb and all. After you neck them for a while, you can really *watch* them losing their brains. You take a girl when she really gets passionate, she just hasn't any brains." (p. 84)

6. Holden seeks and receives advice

In what respect does Holden's sex life "stink"? Comment on Holden's conversation with Old Luce on sex and the "philosophy of the East" (pp. 131–133).

7. How times have changed

Do you think that today's adolescents have fewer problems with sex than Holden had? Refer also to the texts below.

Holden (almost 17):

"I'm a virgin." (p. 83) "... when I'm horsing around with a girl, I have a helluva lot of trouble of just *find*ing what I'm looking for ..." (p. 84).

Today's facts:
Today more than half of the females and three-quarters of the males ages 15 to 19 have experienced sexual intercourse, according to the Commission on Adolescent Sexual Health. And while the average age at first intercourse has come down only a year since 1970 (currently it's 17 for girls and 16 for boys), speed is of the essence for the new generation.

From: TIME, June 15, 1998, vol. 151, No. 23

What parents think about it
Part of the problem for many adults is that they aren't quite sure how they feel about teenage sex. A third of adults think adolescent sexual activity is wrong, while a majority of adults think it's O. K. and, under certain conditions, normal, healthy behavior [...] In one breath, parents say they perceive it as a public health issue and want [...] more material in the media about responsible human and sexual interaction. And in the next breath, they claim it's a moral issue to be resolved through preaching abstinence and the virtues of virginity and getting the trash off TV. 'You start out talking about condoms in this country, and you end up fighting about the future of the American family...'.

From: TIME, June 15, 1998, vol. 151, No. 23

Some consequences
The good news about their precocious knowledge of the mechanics of sex is that a growing number of teens know how to protect themselves at least physically. But what about their emotional health and social behavior? [...]

One ugly side effect is a presumption among many adolescent boys that sex is an entitlement – an attitude that fosters a breakdown of respect for oneself and others. Says a seventh-grade girl: 'The guy will ask you up front. If you turn him down, you're a bitch. But if you do it, you're a ho.'

From: TIME, June 15, 1998, vol. 151, No. 23

A "case study"
With so much talk of sex in the air, the extinction of the hapless, sexually naive kid seems an inevitability. Indeed, kids today as young as seven to 10 are picking up the first details of sex even in Saturday-morning cartoons. Brett, a 14-year-old in Denver, says it doesn't matter to him whether his parents chat with him about sex or not because he gets so much from TV. Whenever he's curious about something sexual, he channel-surfs his way to certainty.... 'That's how I learned to kiss, when I was eight.' And the girl told me, 'Oh, you sure know how to do it.'

From: TIME, June 15, 1998, vol. 151, No. 23

1. Phoniness

How would you characterize the behaviour of the persons in the cartoon?
What kind of behaviour is called "phony" by Holden?
Why do the persons behave like this?

Extracts	Your answers
a) Headmaster at Elkton Hills (p. 12) "the phoniest bastard I ever met"	
b) Old Ossenburger (p. 14) "big phony bastard"	
c) At Old Ernie's (pp. 76–79) "this very phony, *humble* bow"	
d) Conversations during intermission (pp. 114–115) "You never saw so many phonies in all your life"	
e) A boys' school (p. 118) "full of phonies"	

2. "Nice" people

Analyze the following passages. Why are the persons admired and called "nice" by Holden?

Extracts	Your answers
a) The two nuns (pp. 97–102, 103, 154)	
b) The kettle drummer (p. 124)	
c) James Castle (pp. 153–154)	

3. Holden's set of values

Which features are in Holden's view characteristic of phoniness and niceness?

4. Holden's own behaviour

Holden despises phonies, but what about his own behaviour? In what respect is his behaviour "phony" and why does Holden behave like that?

Extracts	Your answers
a) Holden – Mr Spencer (p. 11): "shooting the old bull"	
b) Holden – Mrs Morrow (pp. 48–51) "shooting the old crap"	
c) Lavender Room (pp. 62–67)	
d) Holden – Sunny (pp. 85–88)	
e) Holden – Sally (pp. 112–121)	
f) Holden and suitcases (pp. 97–98)	

5. Your own criticism of the grown-up world

Make a ranking:

1. ______________________
2. ______________________
3. ______________________
4. ______________________
5. ______________________

6. Your main values

Make a ranking:

1. ______________
2. ______________
3. ______________
4. ______________
5. ______________

7. Compare your list of values with the following list

JUGENDUMFRAGE: FAMILIE, WÜNSCHE, WERTE

Bei Sorgen und Problemen ist Mutter die Nummer 1

Was deutschen Jugendlichen für ihre Lebenszufriedenheit wichtig ist und welche Rangfolge sie ihren Werten geben. Wie Eltern und andere Bezugspersonen von ihnen gesehen und geschätzt werden. Für die repräsentative STERN-Studie wurden 12- und 13-Jährige sowie 17- und 18-Jährige und deren Eltern befragt.

Stern Nr. 52 Hamburg, 22.12.1999

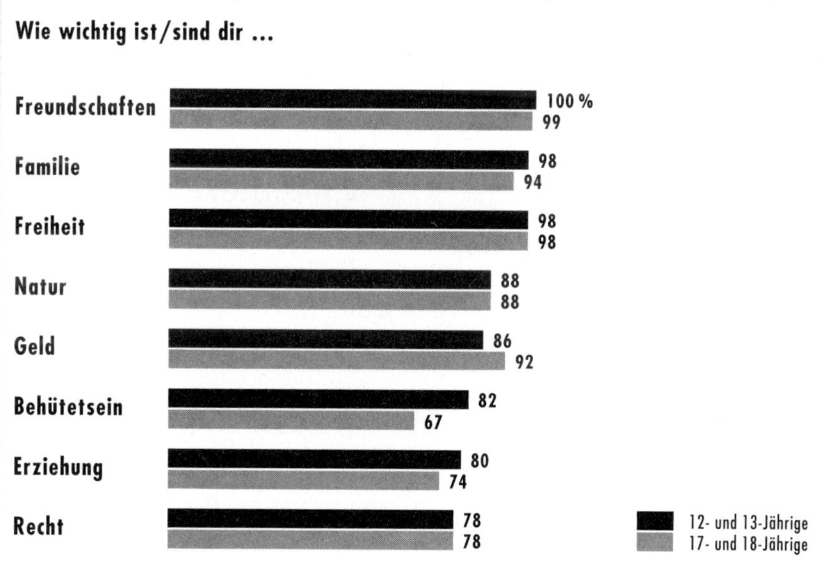

8. Arrange a formal debate on one of the following topics

a) "Should one always stick to one's ideals?"
b) "Should one always tell the truth?"

1. Reading chapters 21–26

Please read chapters 21–26. What are the main events in each chapter and what is their meaning? Note down your findings in the following table:

Chapter	Main events	Meaning
21		
22		
23		
24		
25		
26		

1. Questionnaire

Have you ever thought of dropping out? Make a cross in one of the four boxes on the right.

If your answer was "yes", explain why you wanted to drop out, where you would have gone, and what qualities you would expect in your private "utopia".

	YES	NO
I just played with this idea		
I seriously thought about it		
I almost did it		

Reasons	Place	Expected qualities

Holden also wants to escape from reality. Can you find examples?

2. Museum of Natural History (pp. 108–110)

© Michael S. Yamashita/CORBIS (ym0134440)

Why does Holden like the Museum of Natural History?
What does his love for the museum tell us about his inner state?
Why doesn't Holden go into the museum after all?

3. Massachusetts/Vermont (pp. 118–121)

Write down your associations with the following pictures:

W. Hoops, Tübingen

MEV

What does Holden hate about life in New York?
What are the essential characteristics of life in Vermont or Massachusetts, as envisaged by Holden?

Bilderberg (C. Boisvieux) Hamburg

What essential value is unfolded in the following poem?
How does it link to Holden's escapist dreams about Vermont?

I wandered lonely as a cloud
That floats on high o'er vales and hills,
When all at once I saw a crowd,
A host, of golden daffodils;
Beside the lake, beneath the trees,
Fluttering and dancing in the breeze.

Continuous as the stars that shine
And twinkle on the milky way,
They stretched in never-ending line
Along the margin of a bay:
Ten thousand saw I at a glance,
Tossing their heads in sprightly dance.

The waves beside them danced; but they
Out-did the sparkling waves in glee:
A poet could not but be gay,
In such a jocund company:
I gazed – and gazed – but little thought
What wealth the show to me had brought:

For oft, when on my couch I lie
In vacant or in pensive mood,
They flash upon that inward eye
Which is the bliss of solitude;
And then my heart with pleasure fills,
And dances with the daffodils.

William Wordsworth

▶ William Wordsworth

* Cockermouth (Cumberland), 1770, the son of an attorney; † 1850. After studying at Cambridge he made a long walking tour on the Continent (1790). In 1791 he returned to France and spent a year there. The ideas of the French Revolution exercised a strong influence on his intellectual development, although in later life he became a sturdy opponent of liberalism. His close and long-enduring friendship with Coleridge began in 1795. Jointly they worked on the *Lyrical Ballads* (1798), in which Wordsworth was to treat characters and incidents of ordinary life in the language of ordinary speech, while Coleridge was to concentrate on the dramatic reality of the supernatural. Wordsworth contributed *Tintern Abbey* and other poems, Coleridge the *Ancient Mariner* [...] The volume was the programmatic inauguration of the Romantic Revival in England [...]

Impressed by the beauty of landscape scenery from his earliest years, Wordsworth was eminently a poet of nature. Nature to him was something to be worshipped in a spirit of mystic communion, and the calming and elevating influence of nature he believed to be one of the chief agencies in the formation of a mature mind.

From: Herrig/Meller/Sühnel, *British and American Classical Poems*, 1966, p. 368,

AKG Berlin

William Wordsworth

4. "Out West/deaf-mute" (pp. 178–180)

Discuss with your partner a topic of your own choice by using paper and pencil *only*.
What are the essential characteristics of this escapist vision?
In what respect is this vision inconsequent?

5. "My cabin" (p. 184)

Devise "Rules of the house" which Holden might stick to the front door of his "cabin":

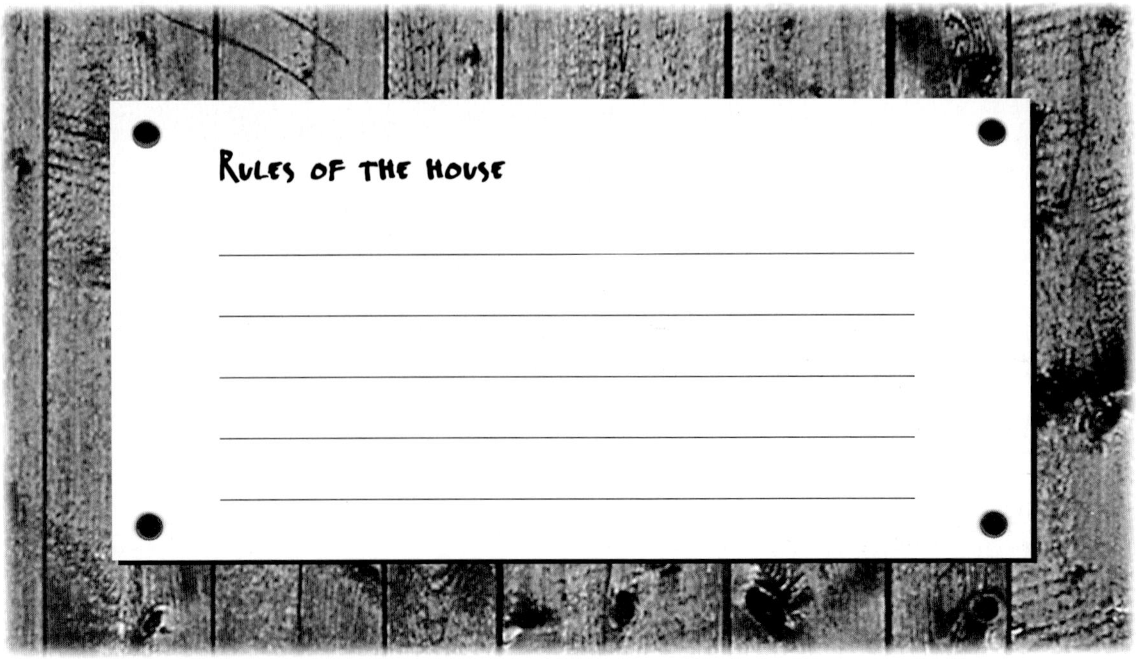

What is the significant quality of this escapist idea and what does it tell us about Holden?

1. The loss of innocence

What relationship do you see between Robert Frost's poem and Holden's "catcher-idea"?

Nothing Gold Can Stay

Nature's first green is gold,
Her hardest hue to hold.
Her early leaf's a flower,
But only so an hour.
Then leaf subsides to leaf.
So Eden sank to grief,
So dawn goes down to day.
Nothing gold can stay.

Robert Frost (1874–1963)

K. Hils, Stuttgart

2. Children in the novel

Collect the qualities of children in the novel:

Allie (p. 33)	Singing boy (p. 104)	Phoebe (pp.143–158)

3. Phoebe's probing questions (pp. 152–156)

What does Holden like a lot?
Why does Holden have difficulties concentrating during Phoebe's interrogation?
Explain Holden's difficulties with being a lawyer.
Explain Phoebe's remark "That isn't anything *really!*" (p. 155).

4. Holden's "catcher-dream" (pp. 155–156)

What is the central idea behind Holden's catcher-dream? Think of how Holden views the world of children and the adult world. Compare the following text with Holden's "catcher-dream". What is the decisive difference?

One idea I have – I want to get a really big house open for kids. Kids that don't want to stay on the streets and get involved with drugs and alcohol. I'd allow them to have freedom to do what they want to do – beyond some limits: no violence – some rules. But not like, "I'm a parent and you do what I say." I want to give them a safe place. I want to be able to reach out to kids and tell them, "Man, I've been through this stuff, I know where you're at. If you ever need someone to talk to, I've been there." It's really time-consuming, not something I'm gonna jump into right away. I want to give myself some experience in learning how to help myself *before I help someone else!* [laughs]

From: Sydney Lewis, *"A totally alien life-form". Teenagers*, New York: The New Press, 1996, pp. 170–171

5. The "original"

Comin thro' the rye

Comin thro' the rye, poor body,
Comin thro' the rye,
She draigl't a' her petticoatie
Comin thro' the rye.
Cho. Jenny's a' wet, poor body,
Jenny's seldom dry:
She draigl't a' her petticoatie
Comin thro' the rye.

Gin a body meet a body
Comin thro' the rye,
Gin a body kiss a body
Need a body cry.
Cho. Oh Jenny's a' wet, & c.

Gin a body meet a body
Comin thro' the glen;
Gin a body kiss a body
Need the warld ken!
Cho. Oh Jenny's a' wet, & c.

Robert Burns

▶ **Robert Burns** * Alloway, Ayrshire (Scotland), 1759, the son of a poor farmer; † Dumfries (Scotland), 1796. Scotland's national poet. At his father's death (1784) he continued farming in partnership with his brother. Bad crops and an unfortunate love-affair with a mason's daughter made him resolve to emigrate to Jamaica. This plan was, however, overthrown by the sensational success of his poems, which, in order to get money for his passage, he had published at Kilmarnock in 1786. Celebrated in Edinburgh as "a heaven-taught ploughman", he settled in Dumfries (1791), as exciseman (i.e. government official collecting duty on liquor and tobacco). Having ruined his health by his association with the hard-drinking gentry of the district, he died of a rheumatic fever at the age of 37. The language of most of his poems and songs is Lowland Scots ("Lallans"), although often not a pure dialect but rather a mixture of Scots and Southern English.

From: Herrig/Meller/Sühnel, *British and American Classical Poems*, 1966, p. 351, © 1986 Lambert Schneider, Heidelberg

1. Two pictures

Please note down your associations with the following two pictures:

AKG Berlin

Piet Mondrian: "Composition with yellow, blue and red", 1937–42

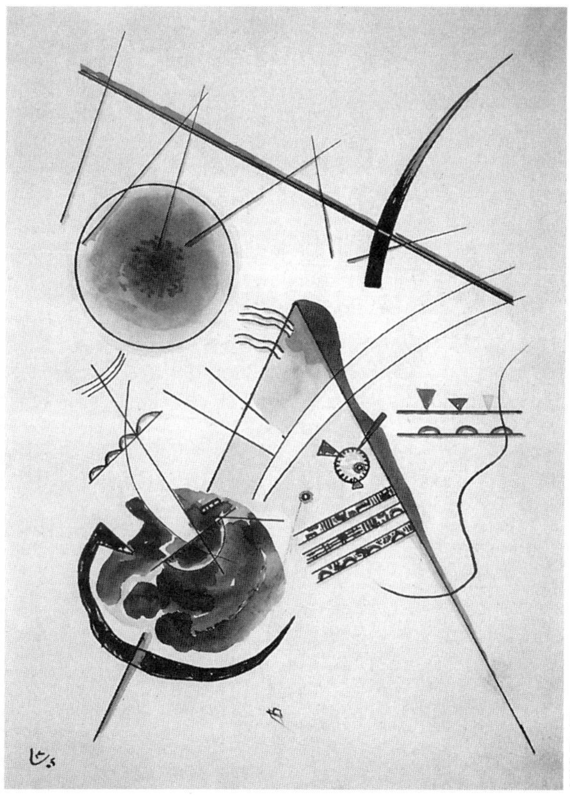

AKG Berlin

Wassily Kandinsky: "Composition", 1925

Which of the two pictures would Holden prefer?

2. Becoming conscious of yourself or: Your "Antolini-level"

Please decide on the following statements and questions spontaneously:

	YES	NO
1. It's a pity that you have to grow up.	☐	☐
2. Is education important to you?	☐	☐
3. People shouldn't make compromises.	☐	☐
4. You can't learn anything important from books.	☐	☐
5. When you go on vacation, do you make plans for each day?	☐	☐
6. One should stick to the point.	☐	☐
7. Thoughts are more important than feelings.	☐	☐
8. Life is incalculable.	☐	☐
9. People shouldn't give advice if they can't live up to it.	☐	☐
10. Do you know what you will do after your "abitur"?	☐	☐
11. I admire people who die for their convictions.	☐	☐
12. I prefer the first picture (cf. above).	☐	☐
13. Do you dislike it when something unexpected happens?	☐	☐
14. I like maths because it is so precise and exact.	☐	☐
15. When making decisions, one should act according to one's emotions.	☐	☐

To find out your "Antolini-level", compare your answers with the following answers: 1. yes, 2. no, 3. yes, 4. yes, 5. no, 6. no, 7. no, 8. yes, 9. yes, 10. no, 11. yes, 12. no, 13. no, 14. no, 15. yes. For each identical answer you get one point. With 1–4 points, your "Antolini-level" is I, with 5–8 points it's II, with 9–12 it's III, with 13–15 points it's IV. Next, have another look at the statements/questions and find out if there is a system to them and predict what Antolini might give for each of the four categories.
Finally, find out the distribution of Antolini-levels in your class by using the table on the right.

Level	Number of people
I	
II	
III	
IV	

3. Being grown-up

What, do you think, is typical of being grown-up?

A ______________________________

B ______________________________

C ______________________________

D ______________________________

E ______________________________

Collect and sort the results and represent them in form of a bar diagram of the following kind:

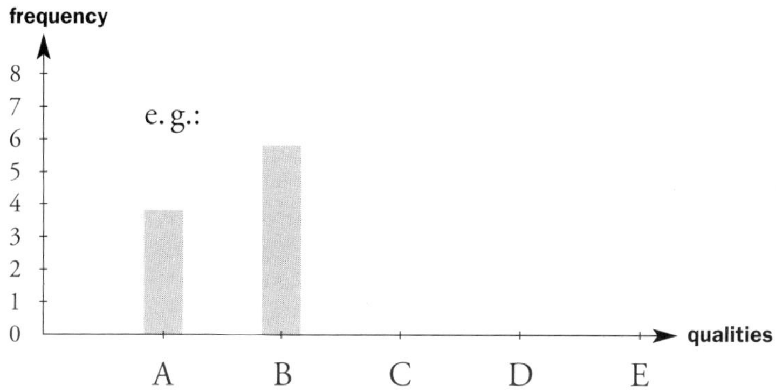

Comment on the results and compare them to Holden's views.

4. Holden's state of maturity

Quickly read through chapters 1, 9 and 19 in order to answer the following questions:
Who said this to Holden or about Holden?

1. "Your mind is immature."

2. "For Chrissake, grow up."

3. Someone said, "that I had no direction in life."

4. "Do you feel absolutely no concern for your future?"

5. "When are you going to grow up?"

5. A digression on "digressions"

Holden says to Antolini: "I *like* it when somebody digresses" (p. 165). Analyze the following text – the beginning of Lawrence Sterne's (1713–1768) novel "Tristram Shandy" (1759) – with respect to its "digressive" structure:
a) Summarize the main event in one sentence ("While ..., ... asked ...")
b) Describe the relationship between the main event and the digressions.

THE LIFE AND OPINIONS OF

TRISTAM SHANDY, GENT.

Book I

CHAPTER I

I wish either my father or my mother, or indeed both of them, as they were in duty both equally bound to it, had minded what they were about when they begot me; had they duly considered how much depended upon what they were then doing; – that not only the production of a rational Being was concerned in it, but that possibly the happy formation and temperature of his body, perhaps his genius and the very cast of his mind; – and, for aught they knew to the contrary, even the fortunes of his whole house might take their turn from the humours and dispositions which were then uppermost; – Had they duly weighed and considered all this, and proceeded accordingly, – I am verily persuaded I should have made a quite different figure in the world, from that in which the reader is likely to see me. – Believe me, good folks, this is not so inconsiderable a thing as many of you may think it; – you have all, I dare say, heard of the animal spirits, as how they are transfused from father to son, etc. – and a great deal to that purpose: – Well, you may take my word, that nine parts in ten of a man's sense or his nonsense, his successes and miscarriages in this world depend upon their motions and activity, and the different tracts and trains you put them into, so that when they are once set a-going, whether right or wrong, 'tis not a half-penny matter, – away they go cluttering like hey-go mad; and by treading the same steps over and over again, they presently make a road of it, as plain and as smooth as a garden-walk, which, when they are once used to, the Devil himself sometimes shall not be able to drive them off it.
'Pray, my Dear,' quoth my mother, 'have you not forgot to wind up the clock?' – 'Good G –!' cried my father, making an exclamation, but taking care to moderate his voice at the same time, – 'Did ever woman, since the creation of the world, interrupt a man with such a silly question?'

6. Antolini's advice

Antolini lectures Holden mainly on four topics, i.e. "digression", the "terrible fall", Stekel's quotation, and "education". Work in four groups; each group should
a) analyze one of the four topics with respect to the advice contained in it and the reasons which are given for the advice,
b) write a refutation of Antolini's arguments in order to help Holden who was too tired at that time to defend his own way of life,
c) summarize the refutations in form of a few keywords and contrast them to Antolini's "philosophy":

Antolini's philosophy	Refutation

Compare and contrast Antolini's philosophy with Old Luce's advice (pp. 131–134).

7. Adolescents with a "direction in life"

Compare the two texts below with each other and then with Antolini's advice. What would be a proper "direction in life"? What about your direction in life?

Gretchen Dee (age 19)

I want to make a lot of money, I want a beautiful house, and children, and a castle, and I want to be able to travel and see the world and be able to send my children to excellent schools. I want that, and I think part of me actually believes I'm gonna have that, but reality-speaking-wise, I know too much. I'll probably have to live in debt, and just make ends meet – especially if I want to work in the political field. I'm gonna drive a secondhand car and live in a small apartment, and probably not go out to dinner, and coupon-clip[1] for the rest of my life. A couple years ago I thought, "I can't settle for that." Now I'm kind of like, "There's nothing wrong with that." I've come to realize that having a job you like is probably the most important thing.

1 *coupon-clip* – to cut out special offers in an advertisement in a newspaper or magazine, with which you get a price reduction when you buy the product in a supermarket

Eduardo Alcocer (age 16)

I'd like to do something that allows me to do not a lot of work but still make a lot of money – like something that fills a need. Maybe a very good script for a movie or something. I might compose a song, a pop song, just to amuse myself, and maybe it'll sell. [laughs] Something mundane[2], in the meantime, while I have the big plan in the background: to write books that challenge the mind, like maybe try to write a novel. I want to write more than a man does this, a man does this, and it's a nice plot, nice plot twists[3]. I don't care about plot. It's more theme-based, and message-based. So that's one of my goals: to make money and do it as quickly as possible, so I can get into the other things of life. […]

Drugs – never. Why? Because one, I was never offered any. [laughs] So that kind of gets in the way. And two, I don't see any benefits. And again, there's the plan. Nothing else matters. I want to get from point A to point B, and I don't want anything getting in my way. And drugs do that. […]

The general feeling I get from other kids is a lack of concern and thought about what's going on. It's like they think, "Why care what's going on around

2 *mundane* – everyday, ordinary, or banal

3 *plot twist* – a sudden unexpected change in the plot

us when there's a new TV show?" [laughs] That's what I miss about being a kid – not caring. The ignorance of childhood, just living for the next chance to play with your toy, or the next episode of "Sesame Street." And as you get older you get more concerned about the world around you. That's kind of the thing I miss – being ignorant. And being able to get away with it.

But I need to do something for the world. I feel like I want to do something positive. It doesn't have to be big, but some positive contribution. And that's part of the plan too. [laughs]

From: Sydney Lewis, *"A totally alien life-form". Teenagers*, New York: The New Press, 1996, pp. 105, 75, 79–80

8. The "flitty pass" (pp. 172–175)

Please answer the following questions:
a) Is Antolini a homosexual?
b) How does Holden react to this incident and why in this way?
c) What are the consequences of this incident?

▶ **homosexuality** At different times and in different cultures, homosexual behaviour has variously been approved of, tolerated, and banned; concepts of homosexuality in modern Western society are in flux. Until the early 1970s the American psychiatric establishment classified homosexuality as a mental illness, but that designation was dropped amid increased political activity and efforts by homosexuals to be seen as individuals exercising a different sexual preference rather than as aberrant personalities. The two conflicting viewpoints about homosexuality, as a normal variant or as deviant behaviour, remain in many professional treatments of the subject and in the minds of mental health professionals and laypersons alike.

The ancient Greeks accepted homosexuality between adult and adolescent males and in some respects considered it a higher form of love than heterosexuality. Judeo-Christian culture has generally perceived it as sinful, and thus homosexuality was traditionally viewed as socially unacceptable through most of Western culture. Nevertheless, sex researchers of the 20th century have found homosexual activity to be a frequent pattern in adolescence among both males and females. [...]

A range of surveys suggests that 2 to 4 percent of the population are predominantly homosexual in behaviour, while at least 5 to 7 percent report some same-gender contact in adulthood; moreover, both higher and lower percentages have been reported.

From: *Encyclopaedia Britannica Online, 1999*

1. Holden's emotional development in chapter 25

The following diagram is to represent Holden's emotional development in chapter 25. The dots on the line represent significant states or events which you are to identify.

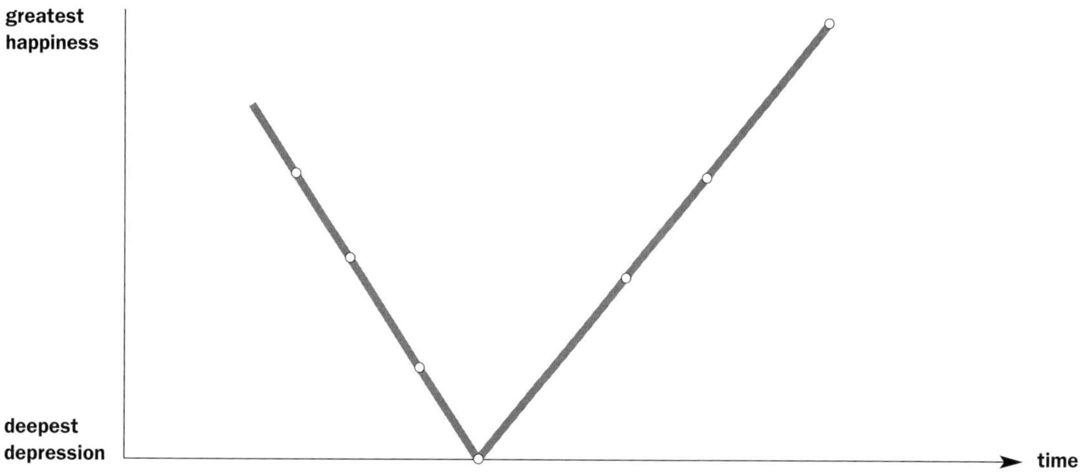

2. Holden's symbolic death and rebirth (pp. 175–184)

The motif of symbolic death and rebirth is quite frequent in novels of adolescence and also central to the rites of initiation of many primitive races. Try to explain the symbolic meaning of the main incidents on pages 175–184. The description of the "Rites of initiation" may give you valuable hints.

"Rites of initiation"
Most of these rites consist, often in form of a pantomime or a dance, of the following elements: The candidate is abducted (and thus separated from his former environment), deprived of his proper name and his clothes (and thus of his old identity), wounded, devoured by a monster (symbolic death), and finally reborn as a member of the world of the adults (new identity). Often, these rites also contain a phase of purification by symbolic washing (cf. the christening ceremony).

3. Holden's change

Compare Holden's quarrel with Phoebe (pp. 185–188) with his quarrel with Sally (pp. 118–121). What is/are the reason(s) for these quarrels? Who plays which role? Write the names of the people involved (Phoebe, Sally, Holden) into the following diagram. Then add a third arrow which indicates the main difference between the two scenes. Explain the difference.

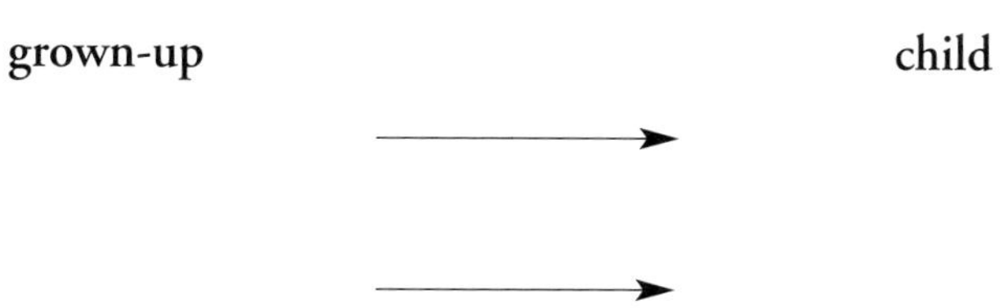

Children's carrousel in Central Park

Holden finally decides to stay at home. Try to explain why.
Have a look at the text – which remark tells us that Holden has changed considerably?

4. The red hunting hat

Holden gives Phoebe his beloved hunting hat as a present (p. 162).
What could this action symbolize?
Holden, sitting on a bench in heavy rain, later on tells us:

> "I got pretty soaking wet, especially my neck and my pants. My hunting hat really gave me quite a lot of protection, in a way, but I got soaked anyway." (p. 191)

What is the symbolic meaning of the red hunting hat – is it a symbol of

❑ nonconformity? ❑ protection?

❑ rebellion against society? ❑ the need for individual identity?

5. Holden's past, present, and future

Holden's past:
Looking back at the whole novel, what do you consider Holden's most important experiences and in what way are they significant?

Holden's present:
a) What can we deduce from the fact that Holden has written his "autobiography"?
b) What can we deduce from Holden's narrative style?

Holden's future:
a) Explain Holden's comment on the "stupid question" (p. 192) with reference to Antolini's advice.
b) What would you predict for Holden's future?

Devise a diagram for the whole novel and add your personal prediction of Holden's future to it:

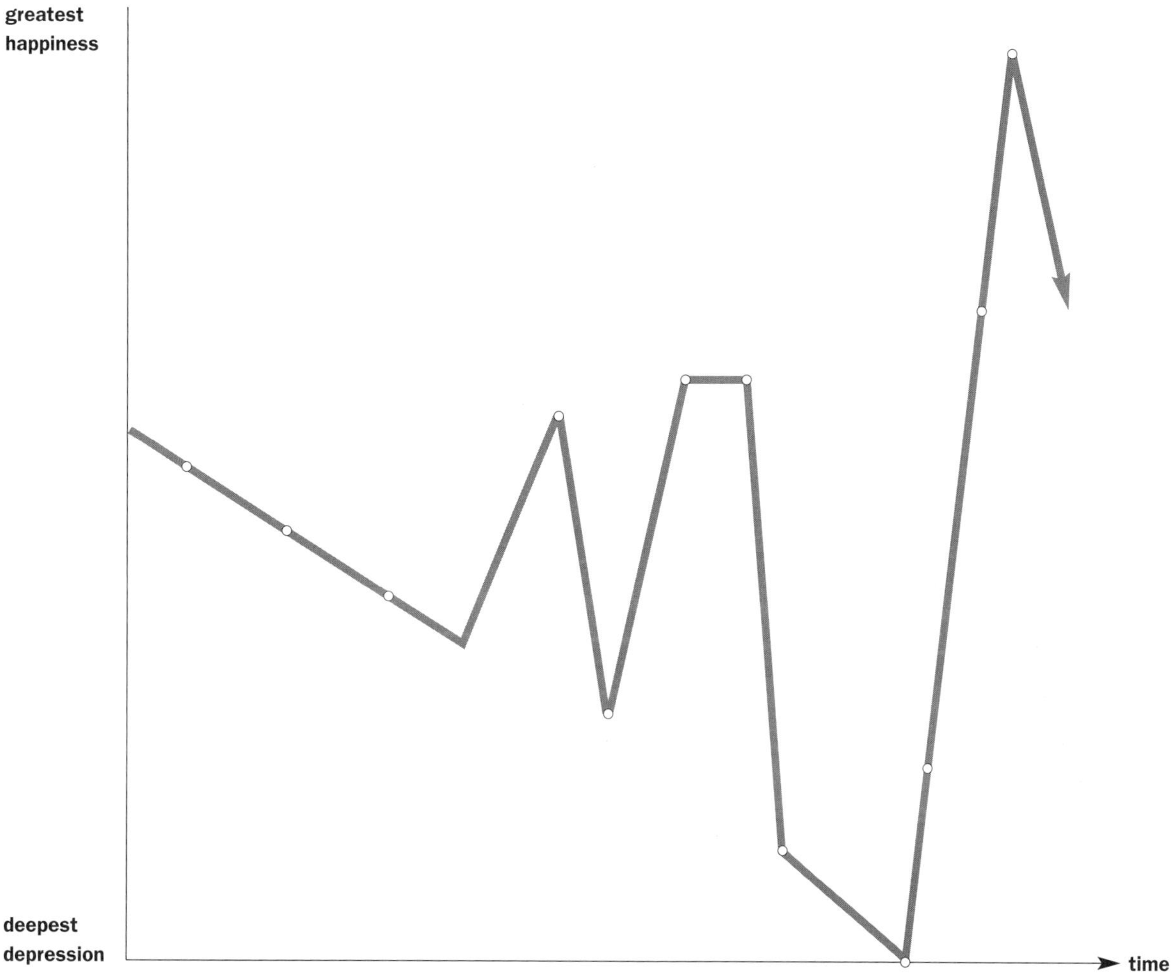

6. Topics for discussion

a) Is "The Catcher in the Rye" more an optimistic or a pessimistic novel?
b) Is Holden's change a positive adaptation to the necessary rules of society or rather a betrayal of his own ideals and a fatal submission to an essentially "phony" society?

> "Like Huckleberry Finn, with whom Holden Caulfield is constantly compared, the hero of 'The Catcher in the Rye' is usually described as a rebel, either against the materialism and ugliness of our society or against the realities of the adult world. But he does not make a satisfactory rebel because he is not for anything."
>
> Rosemary Hamilton, YNHTI, "Dress Rehearsal", Internet

1. Kind of novel

Is "The Catcher in the Rye" more a "Bildungsroman" or rather a novel of social criticism? Refer to the following text.

▶ The **Bildungsroman,** or novel about upbringing and education, seems to have its beginnings in Goethe's work *Wilhelm Meisters Lehrjahre* (1796), which is about the processes by which a sensitive soul discovers its identity and its role in the big world. A story of the emergence of a personality and a talent, with its implicit motifs of struggle, conflict, suffering, and success, has an inevitable appeal for the novelist; many first novels are autobiographical and attempt to generalize the author's own adolescent experiences into a kind of universal symbol of the growing and learning processes. Charles Dickens embodies a whole *Bildungsroman* in works like *David Copperfield* (1850) and *Great Expectations* (1861), but allows the emerged ego of the hero to be absorbed into the adult world, so that he is the character that is least remembered. H. G. Wells, influenced by Dickens but vitally concerned with education because of his commitment to socialist or utopian programs, looks at the agonies of the growing process from the viewpoint of an achieved utopia in *The Dream* (1924) and, in *Joan and Peter* (1918), concentrates on the search for the right modes of apprenticeship to the complexities of modern life.

The school story established itself in England as a form capable of popularization in children's magazines, chiefly because of the glamour of elite systems of education as first shown in Thomas Hughes's *Tom Brown's School Days* (1857), which is set at Rugby. In France, *Le Grand Meaulnes* (1913) of Alain-Fournier is the great exemplar of the school novel. The studies of struggling youth presented by Hermann Hesse became, after his death in 1962, part of an American campus cult indicating the desire of the serious young to find literary symbols for their own growing problems.

Samuel Butler's *Way of All Flesh*, which was written by 1885 but not published until 1903, remains one of the greatest examples of the modern *Bildungsroman*; philosophical and polemic as well as moving and comic, it presents the struggle of a growing soul to further, all unconsciously, the aims of evolution, and is a devastating indictment of Victorian paternal tyranny. But probably James Joyce's *Portrait of the Artist as a Young Man* (1916), which portrays the struggle of the nascent artistic temperament to overcome the repressions of family, state, and church, is the unsurpassable model of the form in the 20th century. That the learning novel may go beyond what is narrowly regarded as education is shown in two remarkable works of the 1950s – William Golding's *Lord of the Flies* (1955), which deals with the discovery of evil by a group of shipwrecked middle-class boys brought up in the liberal tradition, and J. D. Salinger's *Catcher in the Rye* (1951), which concerns the attempts of an adolescent American to come to terms with the adult world in a series of brief encounters, ending with his failure and his ensuing mental illness.

"novel" *Encyclopaedia Britannica Online*
<http://www.eb.co.uk:180/bol/topic?eu=119374&sctn=9>
[Accessed March 25, 1999]

2. Contemporary reception of "The Catcher in the Rye"

Compare the following two reviews of the novel which appeared in the year of its first publication.

New Novels in the News

The Catcher in the Rye, by J. D. Salinger

BY T. MORRIS LONGSTRETH

Mr. Salinger is a war veteran in his early thirties who has written short stories for *The New Yorker* and other magazines. This, his first novel, is the midsummer selection of the Book-of-the-Month Club. A sixteen-year-old schoolboy, Holden Caulfield, tells the story – with the paradoxical result that is not fit for children to read. Mr. Salinger says, "All of my best friends are children. It's almost unbearable to me to realize that my book will be kept on a shelf out of their reach." Many adults as well will not wish to condition themselves to Holden's language. Indeed, one finds it hard to believe that a true lover of children could father this tale. [...]

Holden, who is the clown, villain[1], and even moderately, the hero of this tale, is asked not to return to his school after Christmas. This is his third expulsion and he cannot endure to face his parents, so he hides out in New York, where his conduct is a nightmarish medley of loneliness, bravado[2], and supineness[3]. Jerome David Salinger is an extremely skillful writer, and Holden's dead-pan narrative is quick-moving, absurd, and wholly repellent in its mingled vulgarity, naïveté, and sly perversion. [...]

Holden Caulfield is so super-sensitive to others' faults that he has no friends, among boys at least. He is as unbalanced as a rooster on a tightrope. He asks a girl to elope with him and then calls her names. He suffers from loneliness because he has shut himself away from the normal activities of boyhood, games, the outdoors, friendship.

He is capable of love, for a dead brother, for a lively younger sister, for all young things, as his explanation of the book's title makes clear – an oddly psychopathic one, it must be noted. (For Holden has mistaken the words of "Coming Through the Rye", as "If a body catch a body", and fancies himself the heroic rescuer of children in danger of plunging over a cliff in the field.)

But he is also capable of wholesome revulsion[4] from contact with the human dregs[5], and impulsively seeks a kind of absolution by offering help to others. He hates what is wrong with the movies, and in the end he forgets himself and his hoped-for escape into freedom to help his sister. He is alive, human, preposterous[6], profane and pathetic beyond belief.

Fortunately, there cannot be many of him yet. But one fears that a book like this given wide circulation may multiply his kind – as too easily happens when immortality and perversion are recounted by writers of talent whose work is countenanced in the name of art or good intention.

Vocabulary:

1 *villain* – Bösewicht
2 *bravado* – gespielte Tapferkeit
3 *supineness* – Gleichgültigkeit
4 *revulsion* – Abscheu, Ekel
5 *human dregs* – menschlicher Abschaum
6 *preposterous* – grotesk

Manhattan Ulysses, Junior

The Catcher in the Rye, by J. D. Salinger

By Harrison Smith

A remarkable and absorbing novel has appeared, J. D. Salinger's "The Catcher in the Rye", which may serve to calm the apprehensions of fathers and mothers about their own responsibilities, though it doesn't attempt to explain why all boys who dismay their elders have failed to pass successfully the barrier between childhood and young manhood. It is profoundly moving and a disturbing book, but it is not hopeless. Holden Caulfield, sixteen years old and six foot two inches in height, narrates his own story from the time when he was dismissed from his third private school to return, ill and in a state of physical and mental shock, to the shelter of his home in New York three days later. What happens to him is heart-rending[1]. To many readers some of his words and accidents that befall him may seem to be too raw to be expressed in the words of a childish youth. If readers can be shocked in this manner they should be advised to let the book alone. [...]

The magic of this novel does not depend on this boy's horrifying experience but on the authenticity of the language he uses and the emotions and memories which overwhelm him. Without realizing it he is seeking the understanding and affection which adults could give him – or even his classmates, who are perhaps an unreasonably repulsive lot of lads. But how could they be fond of this overgrown, precocious, and yet childish boy? His roommate was an arrogant hunter of girls; the boy next door never brushed his teeth and was always picking at his pimples; the group of "intellectuals", the grinds[2], and the athletes were all phonies to him. But Holden's sense of phoniness is never contempt. It is worse; it is despair. [...]

He slipped into his parents' apartment after midnight to look at his sleeping little sister and then visited the one teacher he thought he could help him. The man was slightly intoxicated, and he told Holden, "This fall I think you are riding for – is a special kind of fall, a horrible kind. The man falling isn't permitted to feel or hear himself hit bottom. He just keeps falling and falling." He writes out a text for the boy to remember: "The mark of the immature man is that he wants to die nobly for a cause, while the mature man wants to live humbly for one." None of this is any use to Holden, who simply wants to know what makes him find so many people false and ignoble at the same time that he is aware of his own capacity for love. Whatever effect the man's wisdom might have had is ruined when the boy wakes up in the night in horror to find the man stroking his head. Holden dashes into his clothes and escapes. "Boy, I was shaking like a madman."

"The Catcher in the Rye" is not all horror of this sort. There is a wry humor in this sixteen-year-old's trying to live up to his height, to drink with men, to understand mature sex and why he is still a virgin at his age. His affection for children is spontaneous and delightful. There are few little girls in modern fiction as charming and lovable as his little sister, Phoebe. Altogether this is a book to be read thoughtfully and more than once. It is about an unusually sensitive and intelligent boy; but, then, are not all boys unusual and worthy of understanding? If they are bewildered at the complexity of modern life, unsure of themselves, shocked by the spectacle of perversity and evil around them – are not adults equally shocked by the knowledge that even children cannot escape this contact and awareness?

Saturday Review of Literature July 14, 1951

Vocabulary:

1 *heart-rending* – herzzerreißend
2 *grind* – Streber

3. A look at what's in the Internet

Try the following URL: http://members.aol.com/jdsletters/guest.html
(last checked on 17.6.00).
Here are two examples from this collection of letters to Salinger:

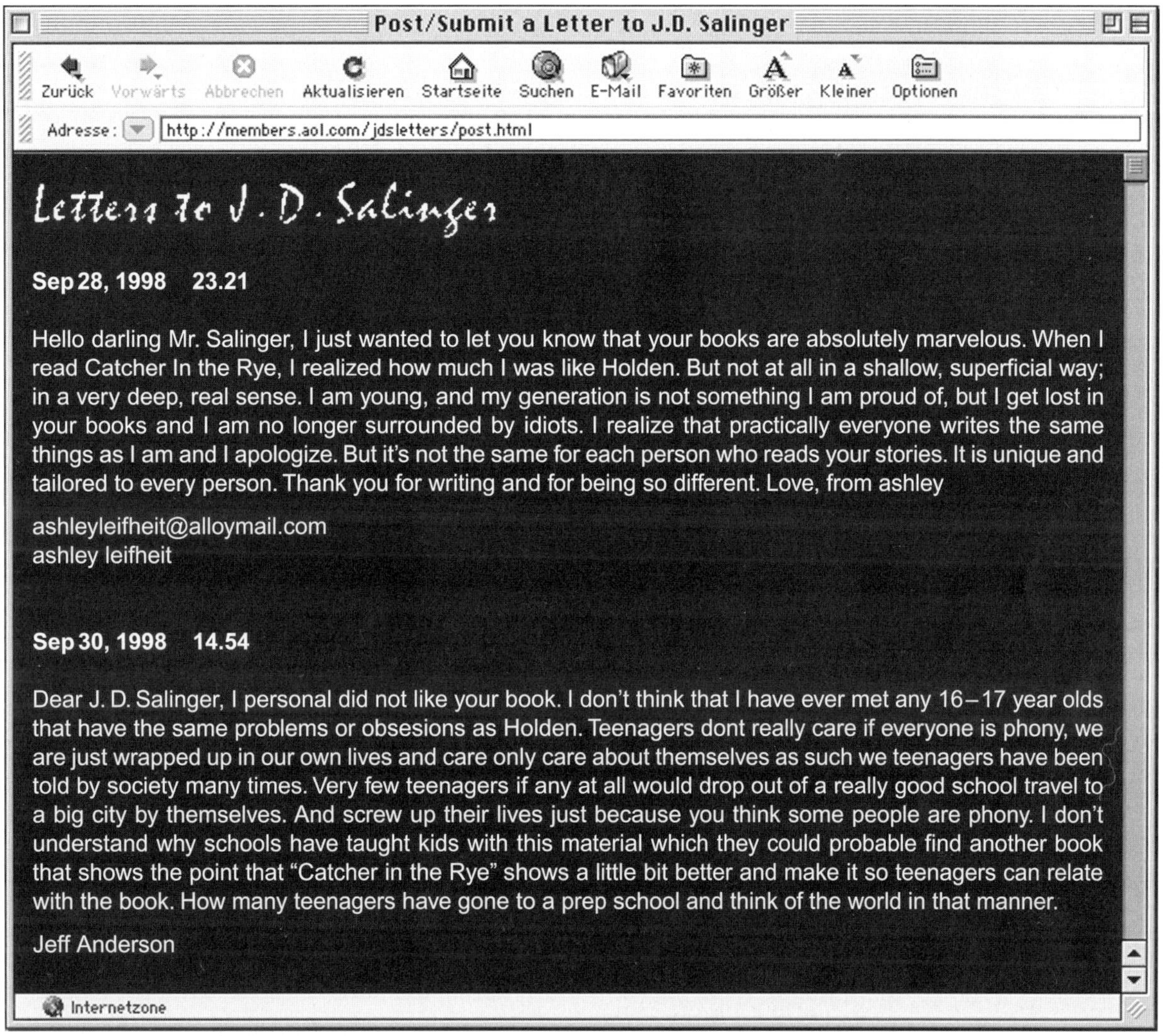

Letters to J. D. Salinger

Sep 28, 1998 23.21

Hello darling Mr. Salinger, I just wanted to let you know that your books are absolutely marvelous. When I read Catcher In the Rye, I realized how much I was like Holden. But not at all in a shallow, superficial way; in a very deep, real sense. I am young, and my generation is not something I am proud of, but I get lost in your books and I am no longer surrounded by idiots. I realize that practically everyone writes the same things as I am and I apologize. But it's not the same for each person who reads your stories. It is unique and tailored to every person. Thank you for writing and for being so different. Love, from ashley

ashleyleifheit@alloymail.com
ashley leifheit

Sep 30, 1998 14.54

Dear J. D. Salinger, I personal did not like your book. I don't think that I have ever met any 16–17 year olds that have the same problems or obsesions as Holden. Teenagers dont really care if everyone is phony, we are just wrapped up in our own lives and care only care about themselves as such we teenagers have been told by society many times. Very few teenagers if any at all would drop out of a really good school travel to a big city by themselves. And screw up their lives just because you think some people are phony. I don't understand why schools have taught kids with this material which they could probable find another book that shows the point that "Catcher in the Rye" shows a little bit better and make it so teenagers can relate with the book. How many teenagers have gone to a prep school and think of the world in that manner.

Jeff Anderson

4. Relevance of "The Catcher in the Rye"

Did you profit from reading "The Catcher in the Rye"? Why or why not?
Would you recommend "The Catcher in the Rye" to a friend?
What are the main problems of today's adolescents? Are they very much different from Holden's?

5. The results and uses of literary analysis

Has your understanding of the novel changed during your analysis of it?
Did you profit from the analysis of the novel? In what respect? Why not?
What, do you think, should be the objective of analyzing literature at school?

1. Parallels between Salinger's life and "The Catcher in the Rye"

What parallels do you see between Salinger's life and "The Catcher in the Rye"?

Schiller Nationalmuseum, Deutsches Literaturarchiv, Marbach

▶ **Salinger, J(erome) D(avid)**

On Salinger, there exist many rumours but only few facts. He was born on January 1, 1919 in New York City as the son of a Jewish father and a Christian mother of Irish-Scottish origin. He grew up in New York where he visited several public schools, among them the reknown boarding school McBurney, and the Valley Forge Military Academy. After brief periods at New York and Columbia universities, he devoted himself to writing. In 1942, he volunteered for the army and participated in the American invasion at Dünkirchen on the 6th July, 1944 (D-Day). In 1946, he left the army and lived as a writer.

His literary work consists of 13 short stories and one novel, *The Catcher in the Rye*, which made him famous. After the surprising success of his novel in 1953 he retreated to a secluded farm in Cornish, New Hampshire, which he has never left for a longer time. In 1955 he married the actress Claire Douglas from which he was divorced in 1967 on behalf of "indifference and refusal to communicate".

His small body of short stories after 1953 is based on mystic and buddhistic ideas and has been criticized as a "withdrawing into a self-referential fantasy world". Since 1965 he has published nothing at all, although he is still writing. In his only interview since 1953, with the New York Times, he explained: "There is a marvellous peace in not publishing. It's peaceful. Still. Publishing is a terrible invasion of my privacy. I like to write. But I write just for myself and my own pleasure."

2. The problem of privacy for celebrities

Discuss the problem that celebrities have with their private life after considering the following article.

Vocabulary:

1 *recluse* – a person who lives alone and deliberately avoids other people
2 *duplex* – *(AE)* a semi-detached house
3 *ramification* – *here:* consequence
4 *to spurn* – to refuse to accept sth
5 *poseur* – a person who wants to impress people
6 *sycophantic* – behaviour in which someone praises people in order to get some advantage
7 *bolt hole* – place where you can escape to from other people
8 *sod it* – a swear word used to express anger and annoyance
9 *quarry* – an animal that is being hunted
10 *prurient* – *here:* showing strong interest

Do you want to know a secret?

Everyone wants to share their intimacies with a TV audience (everyone, that is, except J. D. Salinger)

Television

by Charlotte Raven

Close Up: J.D.Salinger Doesn't Want to Talk

IT IS TEMPTING to speculate what would have happened to J. D. Salinger if he hadn't spent the past few decades as the literary world's most famous recluse[1]. Would he be writing screenplays in Hollywood, or working on the Great American Novel in a minimal Manhattan duplex[2] across the hall from Jerry Steinfeld's? In either location, J. D. would be a respected public figure. His views would be sought on everything, from Monica Lewinsky's lipstick to the ethical ramifications[3] of human cloning. He would go to charity benefits, have feuds with other writers in the pages of the *New York Review* and believe in right-wing conspiracies. Perhaps, like Salman Rushdie, he would make a pop record with Bono.

When Salinger retreated from public life at the height of his popularity, everyone thought 'How rude'. For the people who identified so closely with *The Catcher in the Rye's* narrator, being spurned[4] by Salinger was the same as being rejected by Holden Caulfield. It meant that they were not, as they had hoped, on the right side of the dividing line which separates 'phoneys' from the treasured few who understand life's true purpose. In turning his back on his readers, Salinger seemed to be telling us that we were the hopeless poseurs[5] who 'laughed like hyenas' in the cinema at jokes that weren't even funny; the sycophantic[6] nightclub crowd who clapped 'old Ernie' just because he was a star.

Ernie, it will be remembered, responds to his celebrity in the manner to which we are accustomed. 'Grinning like a madman' throughout his set, he gives a 'humble bow' at the end. He does not stick two fingers up and run off to a bolt hole[7] in the country the minute people start applauding.

Yet this is just what Salinger did. He woke up one morning, thought 'Sod it'[8] and refused to take any more calls. His punishment for breaking the rules is to be hounded, day and night, by biographers and documentary makers demanding an 'explanation'. The producers of last week's **Close Up: J. D. Salinger Doesn't Want to Talk** were keen to reassure viewers from the outset that their quarry[9] was a legitimate target. Far from being merely prurient[10], their interest was founded on a genuine belief that the public had the right to know the truth. 'Like Holden, Salinger also ran away from the world. But what were they both hiding from?' intoned the narration, blind to the obvious fact that a distaste for being chased by cameras is not proof, in itself, that the person being followed is 'hiding'.

At the start of the programme we were shown some 'unique footage' – captured from behind a row of bushes – which demonstrated conclusively that Salinger is an old man. Even more excitingly, it showed that he goes to the shops. It also proved that, whether he likes it or not, Salinger is a celebrity. The paparazzi shot – that symbol of the public's right to impose fame irrespective of the victim's wishes – is all the evidence the viewer needs to put him up there with Posh Spice.

I don't buy all this 'right to know' stuff. Biography is not a public service and I could have managed quite well without knowing what Salinger eats for breakfast (frozen peas, apparently) or where he spent his childhood summers – details that Holden would doubtless dismiss as so much 'David Copperfield crap'. Peppering their story with a great many probablys and may have beens, the programme makers tiptoe through Salinger's life, intent on discovering the 'trauma' that might have caused him to retreat. Their most convincing candidate is the war. Salinger's involvement in some of the bloodiest battles, and a subsequent nervous breakdown, may well have deepened his disillusionment with humanity. But could we really say, as they do, that the war was the cause of this condition?

Surely the writer of *The Catcher in the Rye* had already told us, in that book, why the world was a danger to anyone who couldn't applaud on cue. For the nonphoneys in the novel, the options are alienation, death or madness. Only children are permitted to live authentically. The others discover that it simply isn't possible to keep all your kings in the back row (as Jane Gallagher does) and make sense in a culture which demands that you play the game. Salinger's withdrawal can therefore be seen as a heroic, if flawed, attempt to preserve his own and his characters' integrity. His critics say this shows he hasn't 'developed' or 'grown up'. They said that about the Sex Pistols, whose *Never Mind the Bollocks* was in many ways the musical equivalent of *The Catcher in the Rye*. In both cases, not growing up – refusing to create an œuvre – was the point.

3. Fictive interview

Prepare questions for an imagined interview with Salinger and stage it before class. Your partner, i.e. Salinger, should know the questions in advance so that she/he can prepare her/his answers. Don't be afraid of improvisation!

Picture Press, © Paul Adao

Picture Press, © Paul Adao

Rare shots: Salinger, shopping with his wife in June 1998

How Well Do Parents Know Their Kids?

Barbara Kantrowitz & Pat Wingert

There are now 31 million kids in the 12-to-19 age group, and demographers predict that there will be 35 million teens by 2010, a population bulge[1] bigger than even the baby boom at its peak. In many ways these teens are uniquely privileged. They've grown up in a period of sustained prosperity and haven't had to worry about the draft[2] (as their fathers did) or cataclysmic[3] global conflicts (as their grandparents did). Cable and the Internet have given them access to an almost infinite amount of information. Most expect to go to college, and girls, in particular, have unprecedented opportunities; they can dream of careers in everything from professional sports to politics, with plenty of female role models to follow.

But this positive image of American adolescence in 1999 is a little like yearbook photos that depict every kid as happy and blemish-free[4]. After the Littleton, Colo., tragedy, it's clear there's another dimension to this picture, and it's far more troubled. In survey after survey, many kids – even those on the honor-roll[5] – say they feel increasingly alone and alienated, unable to connect with their parents, teachers and sometimes even classmates. They're desperate for guidance, and when they don't get what they need at home or in school, they cling to cliques or immerse themselves in a universe out of their parents' reach, a world defined by computer games, TV and movies, where brutality is so common it has become mundane[6]. The parents of Eric Harris and Dylan Klebold have told friends they never dreamed their sons could kill. It's an extreme case, but it has made a lot of parents wonder: do we really know our kids?

Many teens say they feel overwhelmed by pressure and responsibilities. They are juggling[7] part-time jobs and hours of homework every night; sometimes they're so exhausted that they're nearly asleep in early-morning classes. Half have lived through their parents' divorce. Sixty-three percent are in households where both parents work outside the home, and many look after younger siblings in the afternoon. Still others are home by themselves after school. That unwelcome solitude can extend well into the evening; mealtime for this generation too often begins with a forlorn[8] touch of the microwave.

In fact, of all the issues that trouble adolescents, loneliness ranks at the top of the list. University of Chicago sociologist Barbara Schneider has been studying 7,000 teenagers for five years and has found they spend an average of 3½ hours alone *every day*. Teenagers may claim they want privacy, but they also crave and need attention – and they're not getting it. [...]

Loneliness creates an emotional vacuum that is filled by an intense peer culture, a critical buffer against kids' fear of isolation. Some of this bonding is normal and appropriate; in fact, studies have shown that the human need for acceptance is almost a biological drive, like hunger. It's especially intense in early adolescence, from about 12 to 14, a time of "hyper self consciousness," says David Elkind, a professor of child development at Tufts University and author of "All Grown Up and No Place to Go." "They become very self centered and spend a lot of time thinking about what others think of them," Elkind says. "And when they think about what others are thinking, they make the error of thinking that everyone is thinking about *them.*" Dressing alike is a refuge, a way of hiding in the group. When they're 3 and scared, they cling to a security blanket; at 16, they want body piercings or Abercrombie shirts.

If parents and other adults abdicate[9] power, teenagers come up with their own rules. It's "Lord of the Flies" on a vast scale. Bullying has become so extreme and so common that many teens just accept it as part of highschool life in the '90s. Emory University psychologist Marshall Duke, an expert on children's friendships, recently asked 110 students in one of his classes if any of them had ever been threatened in high school. To his surprise, "they all raised their hand." [...]

When they're isolated from parents, teens are also more vulnerable to serious emotional problems. Surveys of high-school students have indicated that one in four considers suicide each year, says Dr. David Fassler, a child and adolescent psychiatrist in Burlington, Vt., and author of "Help Me I'm Sad: Recognizing, Treating and Preventing Childhood and Adolescent Depression." By the end of high school, many have actually tried to kill themselves. "Often the parents or teachers don't realize it was a suicide attempt," he says. "It can be something ambiguous like an overdose of nonprescription pills from the medicine cabinet or getting drunk and crashing the car with suicidal thoughts."

Even the best, most caring parents can't protect their teenagers from all these problems, but involved parents can make an enormous difference. Kids do listen. Teenage drug use (although still high) is slowly declining, and even teen pregnancy and birthrates are down slightly – largely because of improved education efforts, experts say. More teens are delaying sex, and those who are sexually active are more likely to use contraceptives than their counterparts a few years ago.

In the teenage years, the relationship between parents and children is constantly evolving[10] as the kids edge toward independence. Early adolescence is a period of transition, when middle-school kids move from one teacher and one classroom to a different teacher for each subject. In puberty, they're moody and irritable. "This is a time when parents and kids bicker[11] a lot," says Laurence Steinberg, a psychology professor at Temple University and author of "You and Your Adolescent: A Parents' Guide to Ages 10 to 20." "Parents are caught by surprise," he says. "They discover that the tricks they've used in raising their kids effectively during childhood stop working." He advises parents to try to understand what their kids are going through; things do get better. "I have a 14-year-old son," Steinberg says, "and when he moved out of the transition phase into middle adolescence, we saw a dramatic change. All of a sudden, he's our best friend again." [...]

That should be the ultimate lesson of tragedies like Littleton. "Parents need to share what they really believe in, what they really think is important," says Stanford Damon. "These basic moral values are more important than math skills or SATs[12]. Seize any opportunity to talk – in the car, over the breakfast table, watching TV.

Parents have to work harder to get their point across. Ellen Galinsky, president of the Families and Work Institute, has studied teenagers' views of parents. "One 16-year-old told us, 'I am proud of the fact that [my mother] deals with me even though I try to push her away. She's still there'." So pay attention now. The kids can't wait.

With Anne Underwood

Vocabulary:

1 *population bulge – here:* increase in population
2 *draft* – Einberufungsbefehl
3 *cataclysmic* – umwälzend, verheerend
4 *blemish-free* – without fault
5 *to be on the honor-roll* – Auszeichnungen erhalten
6 *mundane – here:* common
7 *to juggle* – jonglieren
8 *forlorn* – lonely and unhappy
9 *to abdicate* – to refuse to accept sth
10 *to evolve* – to change gradually
11 *to bicker* – to quarrel
12 *SAT* – Scholastic Aptitude Test (trademark), a standardized nationwide multiple-choice test to determine the language and mathematical aptitude of high school students who want to study at a college or university

ON FASHION

Marisol Salguero, 16
Junior, Alexander Hamilton High School, Los Angeles. AP and honors classes, academic tutor.

"The biggest thing here is wearing name-brand clothes. If you even think of wearing a non-name brand, you have guts. Looks are real important, too. If you're not pretty, people won't want to hang out with you. Even the girls with dark hair usually dye their hair blonde. Everything is just one big competition."

ON MEDIA VIOLENCE

Chris Haley, 17
Junior, Lewisville High School, Lewisville, Texas. Founder of philosophy group, loves classical music.

"Our generation is far more desensitized to violence than any other generation. TVs raise children now more than parents do, and television caters to children's violent fantasies. Parents are working more and spending less time with their kids."

ON CLIQUES

Julia Papastavridis, 15
Freshman, the Paideia School, Atlanta. Student rep on the disciplinary committee, chorus member.

"I see people who don't allow themselves to grow in certain areas, even though they have talent or skill, because they feel that would be out of character or that people wouldn't like them if they changed. Say you're really good at math, but your friends say, 'I hate math. It's such a nerdy stupid subject.' You can't be good at it because then you're a nerdy brainiac person. And then you feel like you don't fit in."

A teenager's plea to parents

Do

- be sensitive
- give independence
- treat us as equals
- say "sorry"
- understand
- make time to talk
- trust us
- deal with problems immediately
- show respect for our ideas
- recognise we are different from our brothers and sisters
- remember what it felt like to be a teenager
- listen and give space
- allow us to decide whether we take your advice

Don't

- overact all the time
- talk about us in front of others
- say "it's just your age"
- be patronising
- bring up past misdemeanours
- repeat everything
- use age against us
- say "you don't know how lucky you are"
- label us
- compare us with others
- be sarcastic
- be angry all the time
- be a teenager – we need you to be a parent
- say "you always" or "you never"
- go on about the other parent to us
- bombard us with questions
- point at us or mimic us
- say "don't answer back"
- be hypocritical

The Guardian, February, 14, 1995

Teens by the numbers

Verbalize selected diagrams.
Find out the data in your class for selected problems and compare them with the US data. Try to explain striking differences.
Write short "expert" opinions on selected problems. Define in advance who the addressee of your opinion is and why you were asked for your expertise.

Demographics

RESEARCH BY BRET BEGUN. SOURCES: CENSUS BUREAU; BLS; NAT'L CENTER FOR JUVENILE JUSTICE; NCHS; TEENAGE RESEARCH UNLIMITED; MONITORING THE FUTURE STUDY, UNIV. OF MICHIGAN; KAISER FAMILY FOUNDATION; NAT'L LONGITUDINAL STUDY OF ADOLESCENT HEALTH; JUPITER COMMUNICATIONS; GREENFIELD ONLINE; THE ALAN GUTTMACHER INST.

THE BREAKDOWN
Teenagers account for roughly 10 percent of the U.S. population.

Teens (13–19)

White	18,199,000	66%
Black	3,992,000	15
Hispanic	3,723,000	14
Asian, Pac. Islander	1,030,000	4
American Indian, Eskimo and Aleut	275,000	1

PARENTS AT WORK
Parents work more, so their teenagers are often left unsupervised.

Families with employed parents

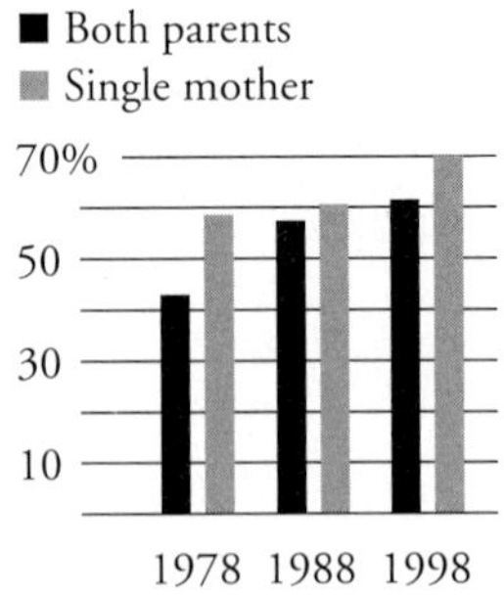

DROP IN CRIME
In 1997, kids were responsible for 17 percent of violent-crime arrests.

Arrests per 100,000 juveniles 10–17

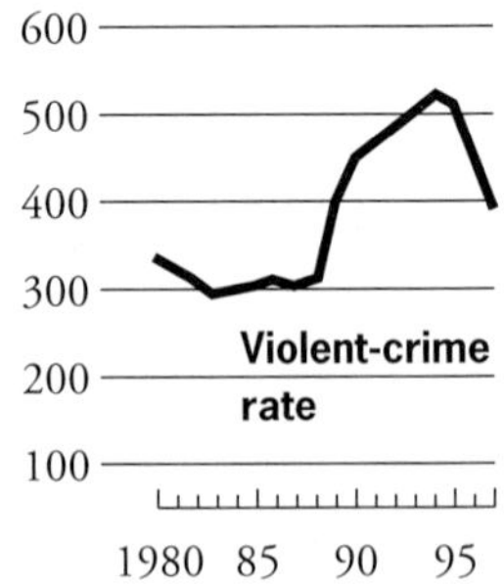

Lifestyle

SEXUAL ACTIVITY
Almost one out of five teenagers is still a virgin by the age of 20.

Percentage of teens who have had sexual intercourse, 1995

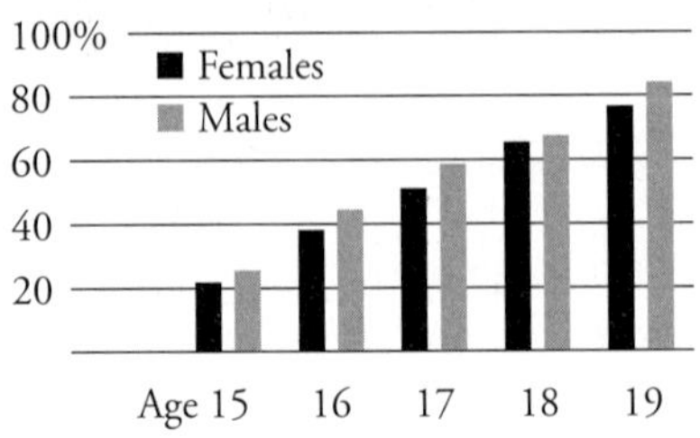

LESS OF THE BAD STUFF: SMOKING, DRINKING AND DOING DRUGS
Today, teens say, they misbehave less than kids in the recent past. The percentage who, in the last 30 days, admit to having used …

... alcohol

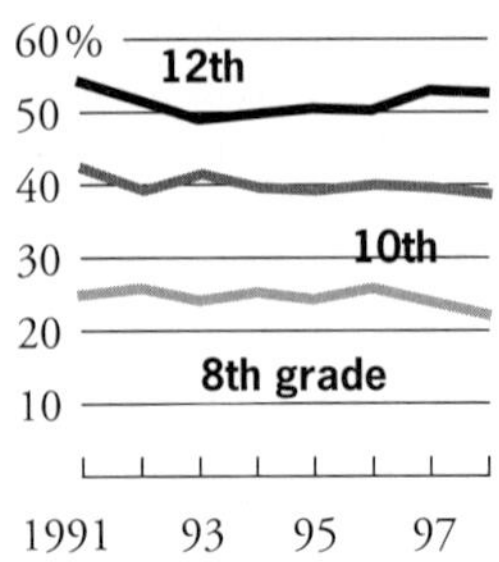

... cigarettes

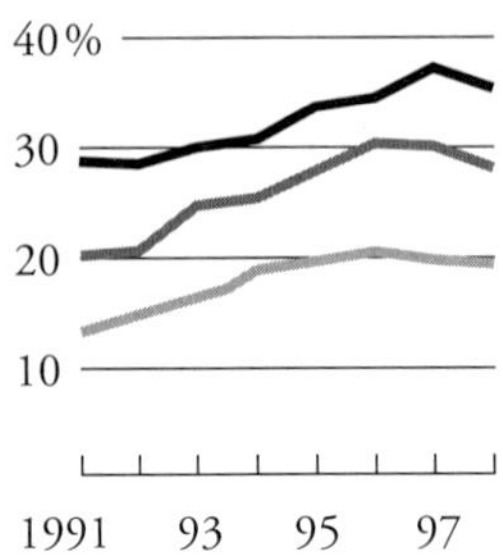

... drugs

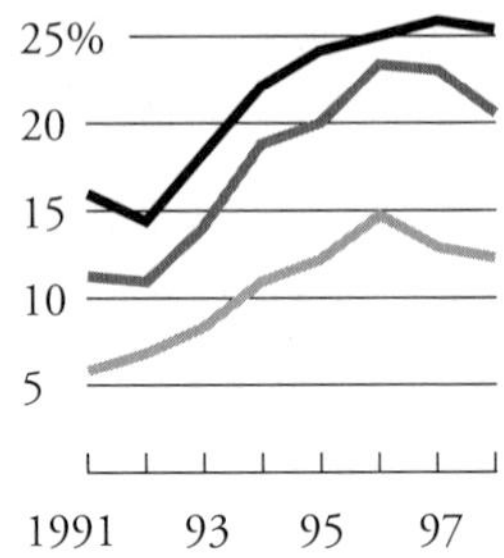

COOLEST BRANDS

Boys	Girls
Nike	Nike
Sony	adidas
Tommy Hilfiger	Tommy Hilfiger
Nintendo	The Gap
adidas	Old Navy

FAVORITE TV SHOWS

Boys	Girls
'The Simpsons'	'Dawson's Creek'
'South Park'	'Friends'
'MTV'	'7th Heaven'
'Home Improve.'	'The Simpsons'
'Friends'	'Buffy the V.S.'

Online

HOOKED UP

47% of teens are using the computer to go online this year.

Percentage of teens who go online

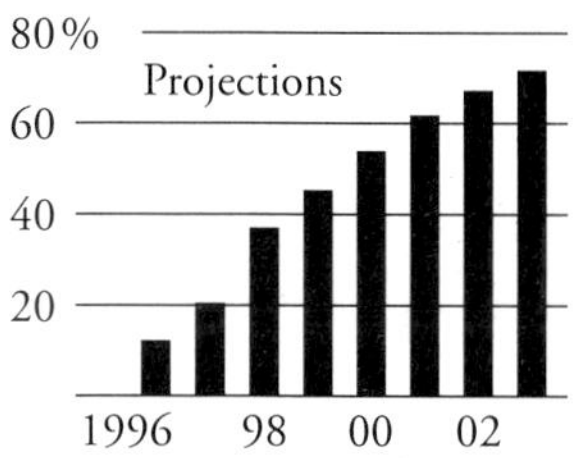

WHAT DO THEY DO?

They keep up with each other – and what's out there.

Top 10 activities

E-mail	83%
Search engine	78
Music sites	59
General research	58
Games	51
TV/movie sites	43
Chat room	42
Own Web page	38
Sports sites	35

EVERY MOVE THEY MAKE

With age comes online freedom. Here's how parents say they monitor their kids while they're on the Net.

	Age 11–15	16–18
Sit with them while online	38%	9%
Kids can log on only with an adult	34	5
Mainly use for online games	28	15
Limit hours for kids' use	47	21
Know which Web sites kids can visit	68	43
Kids are online whenever they want	54	75
Use the Net more than watching TV	19	22

Home life

PASSING THE HOURS

Kids spend more time partying than studying each week. They also like tube time.

Activity	percentage of teens	/hours
Watching TV	98%	11.0
Listening to CDs, tapes, etc.	96	9.9
Doing chores	84	4.1
Studying	59	3.7
Going to parties	58	4.0
Going to religious functions	51	2.5
Working at a regular paid job	32	4.7

WHAT WERE WE TALKING ABOUT?

Parents and kids both say they're discussing important life issues.

Issue discussed	parents	/kids
Alcohol/drugs	98%	90%
How to handle violent situations	83	80
Basic facts of reproduction	76	80
AIDS	78	75

- **85%** of teens said that **Mom** cares 'very much' about them. **58%** said the same about **Dad.**
- **25%** of teens said that their **mom** is 'always' **home** when they return from school. **10%** said their **dad** was.
- Do parents let teenagers make their own decisions about weekend **curfew? 66%** said no.
- How much are teens **'understood'** by their family members? **35%** said 'quite a bit.'

SPENDING HABITS

Teens average just under $100 in total weekly spending.

Weekly spending

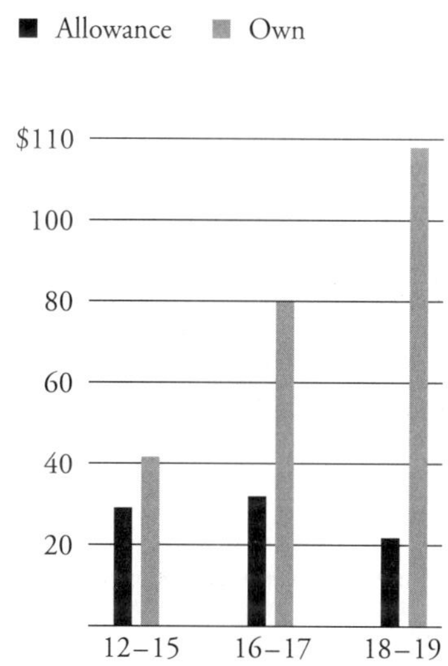

From: Newsweek, May 10, © 1999 Newsweek, Inc.

At 16, they control their lives.

by Martin Bright, Dorota Nosowicz and Nerma Jelacic

But do you really come of age at 16? Brian doesn't see his sixteenth birthday as particulary significant: 'It's no big deal really, I would much rather be 17. At my age there is nothing to do. Every time I go out my dad picks me up and drops me off. When I'm 17 I'll learn to drive and become a bit more independent. But it does bring me closer to adulthood when I'll be able to do the things that really matter.'

Brian has a healthy disregard for politicians and a rough-and-ready plan for reform.

'I'm not happy with the way they operate all over the world. I would make a new set of rules and these would be more strict than the present ones: They would be the same for every country. If a politician broke the rules he would have to pay a large fine or face going to prison. I think this would reduce injustice.'

Street violence, injustice, drugs, guns, all these worry Brian, but even with them and estrangement[1] from his mother and sister, he considers himself happy: 'I have the whole future ahead of me. That is the most important thing to me.

This means I can always make a choice and if I make a mistake I can correct it.'

At 16 you can ...

- ✓ have heterosexual sex
- ✓ get married in England with parental consent
- ✓ ditto in Scotland without
- ✓ leave home legally
- ✓ leave school
- ✗ vote
- ✗ drive a car
- ✗ claim benefit
- ✗ buy alcohol
- ✗ sign a credit agreement
- ✗ be a signatory to a will

CHRIS SMITH, from Frankley in South Birmingham, has his future planned out for the next five years. 'I am going into further education to do a GNVQ Advanced Leisure and Sports for two years. I hope to get into leisure management after doing a degree. I see myself as a career person until my late twenties, then I see myself settling down,' he said.

'Other people tell me I have a very adult head on my shoulders and act like an adult. I'm an instructor three times a week at a martial arts[2] club where I teach adults and have to deal with a lot of situations.'

The outside world has yet to impinge[3] on his career-driven consciousness. 'I'm not really concerned with Greenpeace or the big issues right now. I tend to deal with problems that are here and now.'

FENMI JONES, who lives in a tower block in Hackney, east London, believes that today marks the end of her childhood. 'I'm a young adult now. I'm moving on to college, widening my horizons. Obviously some 16-year-olds are still immature and just don't know what they're doing, but I think you should be capable of making your own decisions.'

Fenmi will leave Haggerston girls' school for a college in the neighbouring borough of Newham where she will study sociology, media studies and English. She wants to be a lawyer. Her parents came to England from Nigeria 30 years ago and both worked for London Transport. One of her sisters is an accountant, the other married to the Nigerian ambassador to Poland. She says she feels exactly half British and half Nigerian. 'It's important to keep a bit of my heritage.'

She feels strongly that the legal age of consent should remain at 16 and doesn't think that the age limit for the purchase of alcohol should be reduced.

'There shoud be much better sex education at school. I had to pick up what I know from older friends, my mum, magazines. Some of my friends know nothing about family planning clinics or safe sex: I know some people mature faster than others, but it's so easy to end up with underage pregnancies.'

She visits Nigeria once a year and was pleased that dictator General Abacha's brutal rule ended with his death this month. 'Now something has to be done to reinstate a civil government. Nigeria has no democracy. It is a rich country with its oil, but people are suffering and I think another country should intervene.'

She thinks it's good to be 16 in the 1990s, a lot better than it was for her sisters. Fenmi's parent let her go out to parties with her boyfriend, who is two years older. If she could change one thing about the world it would be racism. 'People hold racist views even when they think they don't. They tell little jokes or they say black boys are all thieves or white boys can't dance. They think it's funny, but it's not.' [...]

The Observer, 21 June 1998

Vocabulary:

1 *estrangement* – Entfremdung; 2 *martial arts* – *here:* technics of self-defence that come from the Far East; 3 *to impinge* – to influence

Teenage girls. They really are worried sick

by Barry Hugill

BRITAIN is growing up into a nation of chronic worriers. A survey of nearly 40,000 young people aged from nine to 16 has discovered there are few things in life they don't fret[1] about: Be it school, health, career or the way they look, a significant proportion spend their lives in a state of angst.

Teenage girls suffer the most, more than half being unhappy with their appearance, one in three stressed by school and nearly 40 per cent concerned about their families. When not worrying about parents and siblings[2], they are in anguish[3] about friendship.

Anna Chandwani, 15, has a lot on her mind. 'There's pressure to succeed from school, family, everyone. You have to get qualifications, then money, a job. It just goes on, you never get a break from it. You have to fit in – even at school you have to have the right jacket; bag, everything.'

For the past 12 years researchers at the Exeter Health Education Unit have conducted an annual survey of young people. Every year the media reports their findings on drugs, sex, alcohol and cigarette use.

But Dr David Regis, one of the researchers, says this misses the more important points: 'It's understandable that the media concentrates on the bare figures of smoking, drinking and use of illegal drugs but you can't look at young people in just these terms. There are background factors which need to be explored.'

The unit has retabulated the statistics for 1997. The new findings will be unveiled[4] on Friday at a conference jointly sponsored by *The Observer* and Age Concern.

A link has become apparent between the self-esteem of children and their behaviour. Nearly 80 per cent of chronic worriers have a very poor self-image. Those with high self-esteem are less likely to worry but are much more likely to experiment with drugs than those with a low opinion of themselves.

The finding explains the failure of much health education to change the behaviour of young people. Dr Aidan MacFarlane, consultant paediatrician[5] with the Oxfordshire Health Authority, will tell the conference that 'almost all health promotion by the health service to young people, on smoking, drinking, drugs and safe sex, is not effective'.

The number of girls taking up smoking despite more than 10 years of anti-cigarette propaganda is causing great concern. Regis believes the current strategy is flawed[6]: 'Having gone through our database we can now show that behaviour such as smoking, drinking and drug use is related to self-esteem and feelings of personal control.'

'Young people who see themselves less in control of their health are much more likely to smoke than other young people. So, there's an argument for trying to get young people to feel more confident and more in control of their lives.'

'I don't have a best friend because I think it can cause a lot of problems. I don't know if I can rely on them because they are like chameleons, they change depending on what is expected'

Eating, smoking, drinking – and fretting

FOOD Almost 20 per cent of girls aged 14–15 skip breakfast. About 14 per cent miss lunch. Only 10 per cent are clinically overweight but 60 per cent want to lose weight.

HEALTH One in three girls report visiting the doctor within the previous month, 50 per cent over a three-month period. Of older girls, 80 per cent clean their teeth at least twice a day. Almost half of girls aged 15–16 report taking painkillers during the previous week. Girls almost always wash their hands after visiting the lavatory – boys don't.

BULLYING A major cause of worry. Of girls aged 9–10, 11 per cent are often afraid of going to school because of it. Across the age range, from nine to 16, a third of girls are afraid of being bullied.

SMOKING A third of girls aged 14–15 smoke at least once a week.

DRINKING Almost all teenagers, regardless of sex drink alcohol. At 16, 70 per cent girls are drinking eight units a week, although this is well below the safety limit of 14 units, 10 per cent of girls still worry about the amount they drink.

DRUGS There is no evidence of an increase in

Helping them gain confidence would help contain their worrying and, possibly, prevent the development of neurosis as they get older. The researchers have discovered that confident young people, when they worry, often discuss problems with parents, siblings, teachers or friends. But those with low self-esteem keep it buttoned up.

Many young people put their worry down to losing control over their lives.

Koiya Donovan, 12, feels under pressure to emulate[7] her older siblings and doesn't want to let her parents down. 'You need qualifications to make your parents proud of you, to get a job, to get money, to support yourself. You can never stop learning, whether you are two, 15 or 45.'

'When I was younger I used to really envy my older brother and sister because they could do more, but then as you grow up you have responsibilities. I'm expected to follow in their footsteps.'

'My sister got very good A-levels and has just finished her first year at university. My brother is going to law school. I'm going to a better school than they did so I'm expected to do better than them.'

'Even with friends, when you're supposed to be yourself, there are expectations. You have to spend your money on just one expensive item by Calvin Klein to be fashionable. I don't have a best friend because I think it can cause a lot of problems. I don't know if I can rely on them because they are like chameleons, they change depending on what is expected.' […]

The Observer, 28 June 1998

illegal drug use. Only 13 per cent of older girls regularly smoke cannabis and very few use harder drugs. Nevertheless, nearly one in five girls worry about drugs.

SCHOOL In 1992 a quarter of older girls worried 'quite a lot' about school. Now the figure is 34.8 per cent.

MONEY One in three girls aged 14–16 worry about money. Forty per cent have a regular job, often babysitting, during termtime, earning on average £16.44. Even at this age boys earn more – £16.64.

FITNESS One in five older girls worry they are 'very unfit'.

Vocabulary:

1 *to fret* – to be worried about
2 *siblings* – Geschwister
3 *anguish* – great suffering
4 *to unveil* – *here:* to make sth known to the public
5 *paediatrician* – a doctor who specializes in treating children's illnesses
6 *to be flawed* – to have faults
7 *to emulate* – to imitate sb you admire very much

Bilderberg Hamburg

The Secret Life of Teens

Sex, drugs and rock have worried parents for decades. But now the Net, videogames and noholds-barred music[1] are creating new worlds that many adults can't enter.

By John Leland

[…] New technologies and the entertainment industry, combined with changes in family structure, have more deeply isolated grown-ups from teenagers. The results are what Hill Walker, codirector of the Institute on Violence and Destructive Behavior in Oregon, calls "almost a virtual reality without adults."

With as many as 11 million teenagers now online, more and more of adolescent life is taking place in a landscape that is inaccessible to many parents. "That is apparent in the geography of households," says Marlene Mayhew, a clinical psychologist who runs an online mental-health newsletter. With the computer often in the teen's bedroom, Mayhew says, the power structure in the family is turned upside down. "Kids are unsupervised[2], looking at whatever they please." A parent who might eventually notice a stockpile[3] of Guns & Ammo or pornographic magazines has fewer clues to a child's online activities. "We're missing the opportunity for an adult reality check, adult perspective on the stimulation[4] [teens] are getting exposed to. Kids have less access to parents, more access to potentially damaging information." […]

Mike L., 13, from suburban New York, is one of the unsupervised millions online. A couple of years ago his father spied on him through a window, catching him in a chat room where people swapped[5] pirated software. But now Mike has his own laptop and can do what he wants. Like many kids, he mostly sends e-mail and hangs around chat rooms, where he encounters both adults and other teens. "You go in, and someone offers what they've got stored in their computer," he says. "And maybe one of the things is 'The Anarchist Cookbook'," a notorious handbook that includes instructions for building bombs. […]

At Neutral Ground in Manhattan on a recent afternoon, other skills are in play. The drafty, fourth-floor gaming room, undetectable from the street, is a teen oasis, dotted with interconnected computers. By a quarter to four, it is packed with adolescent boys. Robert, one of eight boys glued to the screens, suddenly curses and bangs on the table. "Die, you stupid whore," he shouts. Then, "I'm gonna go kill Sebastian now." Sebastian, three terminals' down, calls back: "You take this game way' too seriously."

They are playing Half Life, known in videogame parlance[6] as a multiplayer "firstperson shooter" game, or FPS. As Robert pushes a key, a red shell fires from an onscreen shotgun; arms fly off, blood spatters on the walls. "If my parents came down here now," says Mike, pausing from the carnage[7], "they'd probably drag me out." The bestknown FPS is Doom; the game reportedly favored by the Littleton shooters, but to the kids at Neutral Ground, Doom is already passé. A new game, Kingpin, promises even hairier carnal gratifications[8]. "Includes multiplayer gang bang death match for up to 16 thugs[9]!", coos the ad copy. "Target specific body parts and actually see the damage done including exit wounds." […]

Most teenagers seem to process the mayhem[10] as mindless pyrotechnics. But not all kids react the same way, warns Dan Anderson, a University of Massachusetts psychologist who has studied the effects of TV on children. "It's always been the case that the kids who have been vulnerable to violent messages on television have been a small minority. But a small minority can cause serious havoc[11]. If you're predisposed to violence and aggression, you can find likeminded people who will validate your experience. You can become part of an isolated group that family and friends don't know about, and that group can exchange information on getting or making weapons." Brad Bushman, an Iowa State University psychologist, argues that violent computer games are more harmful than movies, "because the person becomes the aggressor. They're the one that does the killing."

Vocabulary:

1 *noholds-barred music* – with no restrictions, limits, or rules, unconventional
2 *unsupervised* – not looked after
3 *stockpile* – a large quantity of things
4 *stimulation* – Anregung
5 *to swap* – to exchange
6 *in videogame parlance* – im Sprachgebrauch der Videospiele
7 *carnage* – violent killing of a large number of people
8 *even hairier carnal gratification* – sinngemäß: noch mehr Abschlachtvergnügen
9 *thug* – violent person
10 *mayhem* – *(AE)* schwere Körperverletzung
11 *havoc* – chaos and confusion

Authentic statements

PEER PRESSURE

Gretchen Dee, female, age 19, white

I got involved with peer jury when I was in eighth grade. The police department had this pilot program where if you get caught shoplifting[1] or something – it's a misdemeanor[2] kind of a crime, and you're a teenager – you can appear before the peer jury. And they ask the questions, they act as lawyers and judges. Guilt is assumed; the questions that we ask are intended to establish motivation. We take into account how much peer pressure was a factor, and then we decide the sentence – it's always community service hours. And we assign research papers on different issues. Like, if you were caught in possession of marijuana, you might do a paper on the side effects of marijuana. The whole experience of being there is very scary: you have to stand at the microphone in a courtroom; your parents are there; the police officer's there; and the adults who oversee the program are there. But the teenagers kind of run it. I guess that had an impact, the fact that someone your own age was saying, "This is stupid. You don't have to do this."

We saw kids from the lower-income subsidized[3] apartment housing and from brand-new, beautiful, three-hundred-thousand-dollar homes. It was a really eye-opening experience: it gave me an idea of what kids are going through, of how important peer pressure is. I could not *believe* the effects of peer pressure: "I did it because he said he wouldn't be my friend if I didn't." And they meant it. I always thought peer pressure was something glamorized by the media, and it isn't, it really is there. I hate to push family values, 'cause I think that single parents are fine, and that working mothers are a reality. But the collapse of families is a big issue; and also how affected kids are by not having parents home, how not in-touch kids are with their parents; how the kids didn't think about things before they acted. It was a good look into how teenagers react and work.

From: Sydney Lewis, *"A totally alien life-form". Teenagers*, New York: The New Press, 1996, p. 99

1 *shoplifting* – stealing goods from a shop during shopping hours

2 *misdemeanor* – a crime that is not very serious

3 *to subsidize* – to pay part of the cost for sth so that it is cheaper

SELF-ESTEEM

Gretchen Dee, female, age 19, white

In high school I was plagued by not having a boyfriend – I really didn't have any serious boyfriends until I got to college. I always had trouble in relationships because I was so outspoken. I had a prom[1] my senior year, and I could've gotten a date, but I was too proud to go with someone that I didn't want to go with. And that will stay with me the rest of my life. I had enough attention, it's that no one ever seemed to want to date me seriously. I felt and still feel every day like I'm not good enough. When I meet a guy I'll be like "Oh, he'll never like me 'cause I'm not pretty enough or I'm not smart enough." I'm not worthy. I can say to myself, "Look at your grades, look at where you've come in your life," but it doesn't matter – it's still that rejection.

1 *prom* – (AE) formal dance party for high school students held at the end of the year

All my friends had boyfriends, always. I don't look at other girls who don't have boyfriends and say, "There's something wrong with that person." But I always felt people looked at me that way. Not just boys, but everyone. "Gretchen has no boyfriend, it must be because there's something wrong with her." I don't know where it comes from, but I have to believe it's partly the fact that you turn on TV or open a magazine and every girl has a boyfriend, every girl is a hundred and twenty pounds, and beautiful. You should be thin, you should have a boyfriend, and you should be smart too. The culture tells you also, not too smart, not too self-empowered, not too independent. And you shouldn't be too good either, because that's not fun.

I've always been at the top of my class academically and involved in volunteer activities. I was Miss Involved, the perfect college candidate. But at the same time, I was so hugely affected by wanting to fit in. I didn't realize how low my self-esteem was, my self-image. I still have body-image problems, I have eating disorders. I'm a self-empowered woman and a feminist, and I believe I can do all these things, and I see how successful I've been in my life – but at the same time I am so affected by not feeling pretty enough, not feeling thin enough.

I've definitely changed a lot going to college. I go to a small college in Minnesota, it's known for being highly liberal and highly intense. As a general rule they get students that were social outcasts in high school – the majority of them are out to be different, weird. It puts me in the absolute norm, and all of a sudden I come off as being really good-looking. What I realized in college was how damaged I was, like emotionally, by the silliest things ... Like the fact that I didn't make cheerleading when I was younger, or the fact that I always felt fat, and how that had a huge, huge, huge, huge impact on my life. I don't think there's ever been a time, in the last eight years, when I haven't been on a diet. My perspective is: I am heavier than everybody else. [sighs] I'm not anorexic or bulimic, but I definitely have a bad relationship with food.

From: Sydney Lewis, *"A totally alien life-form". Teenagers*, New York: The New Press, 1996, pp. 101–102

WEIGHT

Gretchen Dee, female, age 19, white

I never enjoy food, there's always the guilt. Guilt, guilt, guilt. If I eat too much today, then I won't eat tomorrow at all. I weigh myself every single day without fail, and if I gain a pound it affects my mood the whole day. I tie food to emotions. When I'm upset I have two reactions: binge[1] or starve – eat celery and water for a week, or eat a whole pizza. I just can't seem to ever eat normally. When I'm in public – when I go out for dinner, when I am at the college cafeteria – I eat nothing.

My roommates were the ones that said, "Gretchen, something's wrong – you're totally binging." They made me get help, they begged me for months. They were like, "We're calling your parents if you don't." Finally my roommate made the appointment. I said, "Fine, I'll go once" – and I went three times. But oh my God, to this day I'm still denying the fact that I have an

1 *binge* – a short period when you do too much of sth, e.g. drinking too much alcohol

eating disorder. Or I see it as, "Lots of people have eating disorders, mine isn't serious – there are people with much worse problems." So when I talk about this it's not me speaking, it's not my true feeling. It's what I've come to accept, and I'm trying to talk myself into it.

How am I gonna stop the "I'm not worthy" stuff? [sighs] You know what is really pathetic? When my therapist asked me that, I answered, "Lose fifteen pounds." [laughs] And part of me believes that if I just lose the weight I'll be OK. Isn't that awful? And I know that's wrong – I know life's not easier for beautiful people. But you get cut a break[2] here and there when you're beautiful: you get more attention, you get taken more seriously. It's no joke that as an overweight person it's harder for you, and that success is sometimes tied to physical appearance.

The media says everyone should be thin and pretty, and I think that's a *huge* influence on all teenagers. There's such a high expectation to be something they can't be. I think they're uncomfortable, they feel kind of dumped[3] on, like the expectations of them are too much. It's the loss of innocence. We have teenagers growing up with adult issues, and they're without all the emotional resources to deal with that. You're still a child in so many ways: you don't have the stability, the self-confidence yet, but you're *forced* to deal with things. There's nothing sacred about being a teenager anymore – you grow up *so* fast.

2 *to get cut a break* – (AE slang) to be given a special chance or opportunity

3 *to dump on* – (AE colloquial) to criticize s.o. strongly and unfairly

From: Sydney Lewis, *"A totally alien life-form". Teenagers*, New York: The New Press, 1996, pp. 102–103

PROBLEMS OF CULTURAL IDENTITY

Lily Wong, female, age 18, Chinese

My old school was all Asian, and I was like, "When I go to high school, I want to be with all different kinds of people." I got here and first I was all, "Wow, white people" – and then I was, "Uh, where are all my friends?", I was like, "This is *too* different – I want my Asian people back." I felt completely lost.

This whole past year, I've just been like, "I want to go back to my roots." So last summer I went back to China on a cultural exchange thing. It was my first time in China, and I felt like an outsider at first. When I went back to visit my home village, I was just, "Oh, God, *this* is what it means to be Chinese!", I was all, *"Yes!"*, I felt within, as one within the people of the village. I felt like now I know what it means to really be Chinese, 'cause I know where I came from, I know my roots, where my whole history began. It's hard to put into words – it's emotional. I was just taken in by everything.

Do I wish I felt more Chinese? Yeah, but what is that? I guess being a Chinese-American, I was kind of torn. I'm not really Chinese, 'cause when I went to China, obviously I'm not – I was an outsider. But then, here, I feel like an outsider in some ways too, cause I'm neither. I feel like I'm trapped between America and China – like there's some internal struggle within myself between these two worlds – and I don't know where I fit. And then I feel like if I hang out with more Chinese people, then I'm Chinese; but if I don't hang out with Chinese people, and I hang out with Sharon and black people, I'm blackwash1 you know. It's something my ex-boyfriend said – he's Chinese. He called me blackwash[1], as an insult. "Why do you talk black, why do you hang out with blacks? Why do you act that way?", After that, I guess subconsciously I felt the need to prove myself – like saying, "I'm Chinese." So maybe that's why I was hanging out with all these Chinese people.

1 *blackwash* – (AE slang) the opposite of *whitewash* (a substance that makes sth white), i.e. a person who is becoming like a black (in the racist sense)

From: Sydney Lewis, *"A totally alien life-form". Teenagers*, New York: The New Press, 1996, p. 123

Jian Bari, female, age 17, mixture of races

When I fill out forms, I put black and Chinese – I check both. I think identity has so much to do with how you're raised, who you're raised by. So I identify strongly with Asian-Americans and Chinese. But I'm black, too, the color of my skin. When you see me on the street you can't deny I'm something – I have black in me. I think the second most important factor in identity is society, the way people perceive you when you walk down the street. I know a girl with blond hair and blue eyes, and she's like, "People look at me like I'm white, but I'm not a hundred percent white – my father's black." And the one-drop rule: you look a little black, you're black, automatically. So it's how people treat you, and then you internalize[1] it. And, I mean, it's not a bad thing, but it's a real thing – that's just the way it is.

I identify myself as black, and Chinese, and American. I hate American, but in fact I *am* American, and nobody can deny that they're American if they were raised here. But America is *so* fucked up and ridiculous – the power structure, values... Our history is *so* sordid[2]. I don't like things like the treatment of Native Americans in this country from the start to the present day, slavery, Japanese-American internment, involvement in the Korean War, Vietnamese War, Persian Gulf War... Our founding fathers, with the exception of George Washington, who was an alright guy – he freed all his slaves. I don't like Thomas Jefferson; I don't respect him, because of slavery. The power structures were white, elite men. I guess the good thing about the Constitution is that it can be amended and changed. And if there were more people of color in positions to do that, change could occur.

1 *to internalize* – to allow to become a part of your character

2 *sordid* – immoral, dishonest, very dirty

From: Sydney Lewis, *"A totally alien life-form". Teenagers*, New York: The New Press, 1996, p. 235

RACIAL PROBLEMS

Akili Merritt, male, age 14, black

I'm constantly trying to do the best I can. Young black teenagers nowadays, when we're at private schools, we don't have none of that Black Panther stuff, we don't have no NAACP[1], or nothing like that. We stay together only to survive, only to keep our blackness. But we don't never make a real change to make the place better – we don't complain. We just bear it and grin it, we just go on. Even in our conversations, we don't talk about how bad the system is, or how bad the school is, or how ignorant these people are. We go around like nothing's happening. We sit there, we joke, we say, "Oh, did you see this on TV last night?" And that's why we're not making no progress.

We feel isolated. In assembly we sit in the back, in one corner in the back. And that's basically where all the people of color are, and the rest of the

1 *NAACP* – National Association for the Advancement of Coloured People, organization founded in 1920 to fight for the civil rights of Afro-Americans

auditorium is white – so we feel segregated there. Where we eat lunch, we eat all the way in the back, and all the white kids are in the front. That's just how it was when I came there, and I automatically went to that area. I think it's ignorance on both parts, and fear of what's at that other table. If I went and sat with the white kids I would feel uncomfortable; I wouldn't know what to say, I wouldn't know what they wanted me to say. And especially with teenagers, you want to say the right thing. [...]

This may be a stereotype, but liberals think that black students in white environments need to be treated special, they need to be coddled[2], and all that. There's this subtle racism that a lot of black people get frustrated about. With conservatives, they just plain say, "This thing is genetics: you're *stupid*," so you can go and throw that in their face. But you can't deal with subtle racism. Like if somebody makes a remark, they don't even mean it, how can you deal with that? It's not tangible: you can't hit it, you can't boycott it, you gotta just sit there and stay frustrated, stay in this rut.

When I first got there, a lot of white people, when they would try to come up and talk to me, they'd say, *"Yo, what's up homey?"* [laughs] Now to them, they was just trying to be friendly, but to me that was just madness! I was ready to knock people out. I was like, *"What?!"* Subtle racism like that: you can't get mad at them, that's just how they were raised. If you do something like yell at them, or punch 'em, then they're not gonna learn anything, they're gonna write you off: "That's just another angry Negro." So, you gotta educate them. I explained to them why I talked like this: I said, "Basically, because when my ancestors were slaves, they were taught broken English to keep them ignorant. They carry it on today." And then they would say things like, "Well, why couldn't you just unlearn it?" And I said, "If you live in a Spanish-speaking home, you're gonna speak Spanish. Same thing with me, what it's like."

2 *to coddle* – to treat s.o. with too much care and kindness so that this person avoids any kind of pain or trouble

From: Sydney Lewis, *"A totally alien life-form". Teenagers*, New York: The New Press, 1996, pp. 355–356

Sequence I: First approaches to "The Catcher in the Rye"

A 1 First approaches to "The Catcher in the Rye"

School is one area where students and Holden have much in common. Before beginning with the first seven chapters, the experience of school is first illuminated from different perspectives: school as they experience it themselves, statements from two American teenagers, and the grown-up perspective on "truancy," an all too common infraction of the rules.

1. School
This task is meant to make the students precisely aware of their own attitude towards school. The table (the 2nd row) is used again in A 4. The individual results should be collected on slips of paper, grouped, and pinned on a pin board and kept for later discussion in A 4.

2. Different experiences with school
Emma Slavsky: *All schools are horrible because students are not seen as individuals with their individual needs and gifts but generally as "deficits."*
Rebekah Evenson: *The Montessori school was good because there were no grades or classes and the students could choose their subjects by themselves and determine their own pace. Performance was not measured with a general yardstick but against the gifts and capacities of the individual student.*

3. Truancy – a way of dealing with problems in school?
I would talk to my child about the latest research results and we could together determine in which subjects there are problems and find ways of improving academic progess, e.g. with private tutoring.

A 2 Reading chapters 1–7

1. Reading the first seven chapters
Among other things students should learn to read primarily to get the gist of the text; that means that it is not essential to understand every word. To make sure however they have got the general idea students should be asked to write a short summary of each chapter. If students do not produce a usable summary of the contents, they can be given the detailed outline on pp. 87–90.
The "special dictionary" might help them to understand the many slang and colloquial expressions.
The answers may vary. One possibility: *See table below.*

Chapter	Person(s)	Characteristic quotation(s)
1	*D.B.*	*"He wrote this terrific book ..."* *"Now he's out in Hollywood, ... being a prostitute" (p. 1)*
2	*Mr Spencer*	*"You don't have to think too hard when you talk to a teacher." (p. 11)* *"Do you feel absolutely no concern for your future, boy?" (p. 12)*
3	*Mr Ossenburger* *Ackley*	*"I can just see the big phony bastard ..." (p. 14)* *"... a terrible personality ... sort of a nasty guy" (p. 17)* *"'For Chrissake, grow up.'" (p. 19)*
4	*Stradlater*	*"... a secret slob [...] madly in love with himself" (p. 23)* *"'Checkers, for Chrissake!'" (p. 27)*
5	*Brother Allie*	*"Allie's baseball mitt [...] he had poems written all over the fingers and the pocket and everywhere." (p. 33)*
6	*Stradlater*	*"What the hell ya think we did all night – play checkers, for Chrissake?" (p. 37)*
7	*Ackley*	*"'Tell me the story of your fascinating life, Ackley kid,' I said." (p. 43)*

Holden's perception of himself and his situation:
- *"They kicked me out ... I was flunking four subjects and not applying myself and all." (p. 3)*
- *"I act quite young for my age sometimes [...] sometimes I act like I'm about thirteen [...] Sometimes I act a lot older than I am ..." (p. 8)*
- *"I read a lot of classical books, like* The Return of the Native *and all, and I like them ..." (p. 16)*

- *"Then I started horsing around a little bit. [...] What I did was, I pulled the old peak of my hunting hat around to the front ..." (p. 18)*
- *"I used to play checkers with her all the time." (p. 27)*
- *"I was only thirteen, and they were going to have me psychoanalyzed and all, because I broke all the windows in the garage." (p. 34)*
- *"I felt so lonesome, all of a sudden. I almost wished I was dead." (p. 42)*

2. Holden in the Internet
Students should be encouraged to visit websites that deal with J. D. Salinger and "The Catcher in the Rye," especially because they can find out how other people have reacted to the novel.

Sequence II: At Pencey Prep

A 3 Holden introduces himself

This worksheet deals with Holden as the narrator. By comparing the opening of the novel with that of "David Copperfield," it becomes obvious that Holden is much more emotionally involved with his past.

1. The opening of "David Copperfield"
The concepts of first person and omniscient narrator should first be dealt with then compared with each other.
The main differences are: *The first person narrator appears more authentic and realistic, he knows about only those things he witnessed or was told about, the selection and order of events and the style of writing can serve to characterize him.* The narrator may be either the protagonist of his (autobiographical) narration or the observer of another person (biographical). In the case of a fictional autobiography, the narrator may be identical with the protagonist (as is the case with Holden Caulfield), or he may be a more mature person who comments on his past life many years later (as is the case with "David Copperfield").

2. Comparison between Holden and David as narrators
Holden and David, two extreme forms of first person narrators, show how different first person narration can be. The way Holden introduces himself shows that he is a rather young person, who is still very much emotionally tied to his immediate past. *(See table.)*

	Holden Caulfield	David Copperfield
Situation of narrator	*In a sanatorium, recovering from a physical and mental breakdown around Christmas*	*The situation is unspecified*
Intentions	*No "David Copperfield kind of crap," only "tell about that madman stuff"*	*Personal history from the very beginning of his life*
How far into the past	*About three months*	*Many years, nothing exact*
Emotional state of narrator	*Very emotional, open, direct, strong likes and dislikes, concern for his family*	*Composed, slightly ironic*
Language and narrative technique	*Imprecise, frequent use of slang, allusions*	*Long, well-formed sentences, great range of vocabulary*
Relationship to reader	*Addresses the reader directly seeks communication*	*Reader is not addressed directly, his/her curiosity is aroused, uncertainty as to the outcome of the protagonist*
General characterization of the two narrators	*Very emotionally involved, language spontaneous and disjointed, wants to get rid of inner tension*	*Mature person who sums up his life in a controlled and humorous manner*

Dickens: *Immense popularity, read by the poor and the rich, able to describe human foibles with gentle humour, given to social criticism.*

A 4 Holden's attitude towards school

This worksheet seeks to compare the experiences of students with the fictional experiences of Holden. The discussion that may ensue after completing the first two assignments will no doubt reveal how pertinent Holden's perceptions are to the present.

1. Prep Schools
The assignment may help students to realize what kind of school Holden attends.

- Values: *inquiry, reflection, analysis; creativity in diverse fields; a winning attitude in all fields; respect for others; profound understanding of oneself, others and the world.*
- Statement of goals: This task calls for students to use their imagination. They can start with the short "statement of goals," which Holden quotes on p. 2. More "statement of goals" can be found on the Internet: http://web66.umn.edu/schools.html.

2. Holden on school
Students can now complete the table they started working on in A 1. *(See table.)*

Aspects of school	Your opinion	Holden's opinion
school in general		*A terrible place*
teachers		*Most teachers are "phonies"*
school subjects in general		*Most of them are boring*
favourite subjects		*English and Sport*
evaluation of one's own performance		*Very poor because I didn't attend*
schoolmates		*Mostly mean or "phony guys" (cf. p. 151)*

3. Discussion about school
The discussion can deal with different aspects of school and should refer to the materials discussed before in A 1.

Topics: *Marks (Should they be abolished?), teachers (How should teachers behave?), subjects (Which should be abolished, changed or introduced?), school in general (Is school still necessary or should it be replaced by courses via Internet?), our school (What could be improved?), motivation (What could be done to make people like Holden more interested in school?).*

Form of discussion: Either a general discussion with alternating chair-persons or a panel discussion with different experts, etc.
For the dialogue "Holden – mother" cf. page 45: "My mother gets very hysterical. She's not too bad after she gets something thoroughly digested ..."

A 5

A 5 Holden and his relationship to other people

Holden's inability to have "a normal" relationship with adults or people of his age is one reason for his problems. The two people he likes are either dead (Brother Allie) or immature (Jane, as Holden sees her). Other people on the other hand see *him* as an immature, weird or childish (cf. his "horsing around" etc.).

1. Holden meeting other people

This assignment is meant as a light hearted introduction to the main characters of the first seven chapters and may serve as an impetus for further discussion about the characters. The roles can be prepared at home. Students should determine how convincing the performances are and not so much concern themselves with how skillful the acting was.

2. Holden on other people *(See table.)*

Mr Spencer	Ackley	Stradlater
Not too bad, but too old. Can be quite brutal. No real contact possible.	*A nasty, slovenly "guy" with a lot of pimples, a terrible personality, and "lousy" manners.*	*A "slob," madly in love with himself, preoccupied with himself, a womanizer.*

Brother Allie	Jane Gallagher
A very nice and intelligent person, with beautiful red hair and a poetic turn of mind.	*A lovely girl with a bad childhood. She is nice to play checkers with. He is very fond of her.*

Holden likes young, innocent and attentive people with good manners and dislikes inattentive, slovenly or egotistical people.

3. Other people on Holden

The students are to imagine that a psychiatrist in the hospital wants to help Holden and wants to know more about him. He interviews three persons who know Holden fairly well (Mr Spencer, Ackley, Stradlater).
The students form four groups (A–D): A = Mr Spencer, B = Ackley, C = Stradlater, D = psychiatrist. The psychiatrist group works out the questions they are going to ask the three groups. Meanwhile Groups A–C discuss "their" attitude towards Holden and their evaluation of him.
Activity in front of the class: A member of group D asks a member of group A, B, and C about Holden. After these interviews the "psychiatrist" prepares a short report on Holden together with his/her group, e.g.: *All three persons I interviewed agree that Holden is very immature. His teacher, Mr Spencer, thinks that Holden takes school (and life) too lightly. In addition Holden's two schoolmates consider Holden to be a weird, unpredictable, slightly insane fellow. In sexual matters, Holden seems to be rather naive.*
(See diagram.)

Mr Spencer	Ackley	Stradlater
A nice but immature student who has not yet understood the rules of life and who does not apply himself enough in school.	*A weird, immature boy who wants to do funny things like playing Canasta in the middle of the night and asks silly questions.*	*An immature and strange boy, who plays checkers with girls and is not able to do things in the way he is told, e.g. to write a "descriptive composition."*

A 6 Holden's situation

Some of Holden's problems and manner of behaviour are quite typical of adolescence as described in the article on "adolescence." Lucy Anderson's statement is a comfirmation of Holden's own feeling of being suspended between childhood and adulthood.

1. Holden's situation and character

School	*kicked out of school for the fourth time*
Everyday life	*absent-minded: lost fencing equipment*
Last day	*series of frustrations*
Social	*isolated, no friends*
Emotional	*lonely, depressed*
Self-evaluation	*ambivalent: child vs. grown-up*
Opinions of others	*needs to grow up*
Dislikes	*phoniness, slovenly people, school, Hollywood, movies*
Values ("likes")	*English literature, poetry*

After completing the table students can be asked to write a letter to a friend. They should sum up all the information about Holden they have gathered so far.

2. Holden – a typical adolescent?

Adolescents typically have problems with …
(See diagram below.)
Discussion: Using the diagram students should explain in what respect Holden can be seen as a typical adolescent with examples from the chapters they have read so far.

3. "Being in the middle"

This authentic text has obvious parallels to Holden's disorientation and at the same time provides specific examples of the theories expounded in the article on adolescence.

4. Holden's short "holiday" in New York

Here, students are asked to identify with Holden and to develop their own plans, which can be later compared to what Holden actually does.

A 7 Reading chapters 8–20

The photo and the street map direct students' attention to the setting in the following 13 chapters. The impressive skyline of the city and what students might associate with it will no doubt be in sharp contrast with Holden's perception of the city revealed in the following chapters. Students could gather more information about New York (photos, street maps, travel guides etc.) when reading the following chapters.

Students will need at least one week to read the 94 pages. They should begin with these pages even while dealing with the first seven chapters. The worksheet "Reading chapters 8–20" can be used by students as a kind of guide that will induce them to read these chapters with special attention to themes and problems. Later on, these notes may help students to find episodes which are part of the same theme or problem. They will then realize that the analysis of the novel needn't always be congruent with the sequence of events in the novel.

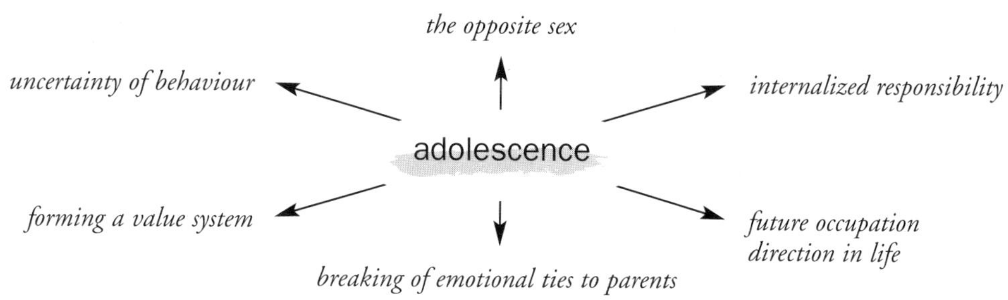

A 8

Sequence III: In New York

A 8 "Trying to have an intelligent conversation" – Holden's search for communication

One of Holden's central problems is finding an adequate means of communicating with others. At Pencey Prep he completely failed with his fellow students. In New York, away from his familiar social surroundings, this problem becomes even more acute. The first two assignments aim at sensitizing students to the problem of communication.

1. What could the two pictures symbolize?
A phone booth [American English!] is a means of communication and can therefore serve as a symbol of communication. A phone booth with the telephone receiver hanging down could symbolize a failure of communication, either because the phone booth is out of order, or the other person did not answer, or the caller was frustrated.

2. Aims of communication
Communication can have diverse aims, e.g.:
- *search for or retention of social contact*
- *manipulation of partner by means of persuasion or threat*
- *search for information, help or advice*
- *settling of business matters*

3. Holden on his arrival in New York
When Holden arrives in New York the first thing he does is go to a phone booth. His feeling of isolation is thus demonstrated. In addition this feeling of isolation is made even more evident when he says "I couldn't think of anybody to call up." (p. 53) His problem is not only his present situation in New York but also a lack of communication. The only three people he can think of to phone are women (Phoebe, Jane, and Sally), apparently he has no friends. Two of them he doesn't phone because he is afraid of their parents. It's too late to phone Jane. In desperation he calls up a girl he has never seen before.

4. Holden in conversation
Answers: *1. Sally, p. 120, 2. Stradlater, p. 37, 3. taxi-driver, p. 54, 4. Old Luce, p. 133, 5. Sunny, p. 85, 6. Ackley, p. 43, 7. Old Luce, p. 130, 8. Mrs Morrow, p. 50.*
Holden's reactions can be grouped as follows:
- *Aggressiveness: Quotations no. 1, 4, 6*
- *Naïveté: Quotations no. 2 + 3*
- *Provocation: no. 7*
- *Playing the grown-up: no. 5 + 8. This is particularly comic in the case of the prostitute Sunny (Note also the irony of the name).*

These quotations demonstrate the fallacy of Holden's self-perception in his social milieu.

5. Analysis of "Holden-dialogues"
(See table.)

Holden's attitude to partner	*to Ackley: He despises him* *to Sally: He loves her more or less but despises her at the same time as the "queen of phonies"* *to Old Luce: He admires him for his intelligence and his knowledge about sexual matters*
Holden's aim(s)/purpose	*re Ackley: He hopes to escape his loneliness* *re Sally: He looks for a partner to elope with* *re Old Luce: He wants advice on sexual problems*
Holden's behaviour during conversation	*towards Ackley: He "fools around," is offensive and derisive, and asks silly questions* *towards Sally: He is at first very enthusiastic, but when Sally quarrels, he becomes very offensive* *towards Old Luce: Holden is vague and occasionally too personal, as he realizes himself*
Reactions of Holden's partner	*Ackley: He feels disturbed and offended, and is annoyed* *Sally: She is deeply offended* *Old Luce: He feels troubled by this typical "Caulfield conversation" and criticizes him for being immature*
Result	*re Ackley: He doesn't achieve his aim and leaves* *re Sally: Total failure, loss of a friend* *re Old Luce: Total failure*

6. Holden could have done better!
Students sometimes find it very difficult to write dialogues if they are not given concrete guidelines. There is, however, a method which makes it easier for the students to accomplish this task.
Form groups of six students. Each student has a sheet of paper and writes down a statement a character might start the conversation with. Then all students pass on their sheets to their partner to the right, who makes some kind of a response to this statement. Then the sheet is passed on to the next person to the right. This procedure can go on for about fifteen or twenty minutes. At the end each group has got six different dialogues.

A 9 "Sex is something I really don't understand" – Love and sex

The problem of finding a balance between feelings and sexuality (or of sex and love), is evident with Holden and adolescents in general.

1. Love and relationship
The picture of the young couple can lead to a general discussion about love and relationships and how they pertain to Holden.

2. Holden's relationship with Jane Gallagher
The relationship between Holden and Jane is marked by innocence – they used to play checkers "all the time" (pp. 27, 28, 37) and, as Holden tells us later, tennis and golf (p. 69). Compare Stradlater: "'What the hell ya think we did all night – play checkers, for Chrissake?'" (p. 37) Their relationship is quite intimate without being physical. "I don't mean it was anything physical or anything – it wasn't ..." (p. 69). Only once, they came "close to necking" (p. 70).
Stradlater, this "very sexy bastard" (p. 28), has a date with Jane. Holden's reaction is extremely emotional and aggressive, for mainly two reasons:
1. He is jealous.
2. He is confronted with sex, a topic he hasn't come to terms with yet. Cf.: "Sex is something I really don't understand."
Stradlater's date with Jane is a great shock for Holden (cf. p. 43) and one of the reasons why he leaves Pencey Prep.
Three times Holden avoids talking with Jane because he suspects that the problem of sex will destroy their relationship. The following assignment looks further into this problem.

3. A meeting that never took place
Main topics/questions could be:
– *"Do you still love me?" This question can be asked by both.*
– *"Did you sleep with Stradlater?" If so, the meeting could end in a terrible quarrel, if not, they might play checkers again or perhaps Jane seduces Holden or vice versa.*

4. Holden on sex
Holden makes some very disturbing discoveries about his own attitude towards sex:
1) Sex is both disgusting and alluring for him. The same is true of pornography.
2) Even a stupid or ugly girl can arouse his desire.
3) You may desire a girl, even if you do not like her. But cf. p. 133: "I can never get really sexy ... with a girl I don't like a lot."
4) Sex may endanger one's self-control.
To sum up: *Sex can be very unsettling and contradictory and needs to be properly incorporated into one's psyche.*

5. Sex and brains
Girls can become irrational when sexually aroused. This lose of control is also true of Holden.

6. Holden seeks and receives advice
Holden's sex life "stinks" because he doesn't come to terms with his sexuality.
Old Luce's advice: Sex (or love) is a physical and a spiritual experience.

7. How times have changed
The discussion can include a selection of some or all of the texts given. The second and the third texts could be very personal for some students. It would be better to first have discussions within the groups. The results can then be reported and discussed in class.

A 10 "Then I watched the phonies for a while" – Phoniness

Phoniness is a central problem in life, not only for adolescents. It has become an everyday occurrence in the media to see supposed enemies shaking hands with a smile. The experience of phoniness in the adult world is in painful contrast to the search for an adequate system of values that adolescents are looking for.

1. Phoniness

The expression "phoniness" is introduced with the help of the cartoon – the central topic of the following assignments. *(See table.)*

Extracts	Your answers
a) Headmaster at Elkton Hills (p. 12) "the phoniest bastard I ever met"	*Calculating, socially selective with his charm. Is only interested in socially important people.*
b) Old Ossenburger (p. 14) "big phony bastard"	*Vanity; presents himself as a 'regular boy' and, at the same time very pious. Wants to be a role model for the boys.*
c) At Old Ernie's (pp. 76–79) "this very phony, *humble* bow"	*Old Ernie: hypocrisy, show-off. Plays a role. Wants to live up to the ideal of a very good yet humble piano player. Audience: plays a role too, wants to be 'in' and admired as connoisseurs.*
d) Conversations during intermission (pp. 114–115) "You never saw so many phonies in all your life"	*Show-off, blasé, conceited. People want to be admired for various reasons: Knowledge, intellectual capacity, large circle of acquaintances etc.*
e) A boys' school (p. 118) "full of phonies"	*Snobby, superficial, elitist*

2. "Nice" people

Extracts	Your answers
a) The two nuns (pp. 97–102, 103, 154)	*They are sincere, modest, friendly, charitable only for charity's sake*
b) The kettle drummer (p. 124)	*Modest, does his job well, is content with his relatively insignificant task*
c) James Castle (pp. 153–154)	*Courageous, doesn't take remarks back, sticks to his opinion even when confronted with violence*

3. Holden's set of values

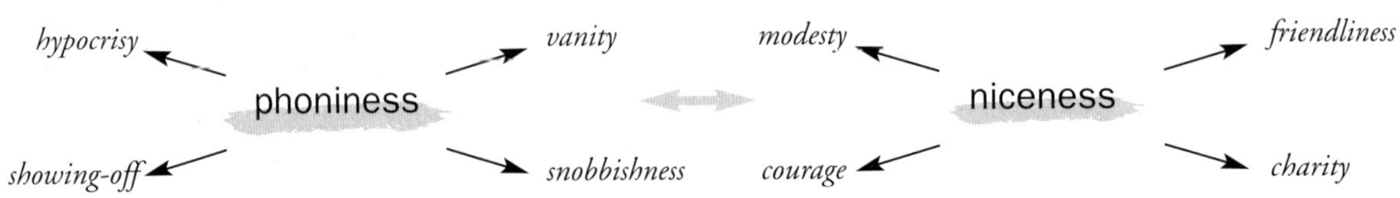

4. **Holden's own behaviour**

Extracts	Your answers
a) Holden – Mr Spencer (p. 11): "shooting the old bull"	*Pretends to understand Mr Spencer etc., wants to help him in spite of his scruples*
b) Holden – Mrs Morrow (pp. 48–51) "shooting the old crap"	*Presents a false image of her son in order to be liked by her, adopts false identity (Rudolf Schmidt) to avoid long explanations and invents a tumor to explain his absence from school*
c) Lavender Room (pp. 62–67)	*Adopts false identity*
d) Holden – Sunny (pp. 85–88)	*Adopts false identity, lies about his age and pretends to be ill in order to bring an awkward situation to a decent conclusion*
e) Holden – Sally (pp. 112–121)	*Makes a date with a girl that gives him "a pain in the ass" and tells her that he loves her*
f) Holden and suitcases (pp. 97–98)	*He is snobby about suitcases and can get quite upset about cheap suitcases. He knows his weakness but can't help it.*

To sum up: *For the most part Holden lies about himself in order to be accepted as a grown-up and to deal with awkward situations. His ambiguous attitude towards Sally is less a case of phoniness but rather the result of his own inner struggle: sexual desire versus the search for a partner whose personality he can accept completely: emotionally, intellectually, and physically.*

Assignments 5.–8.
These assignments serve to make students more aware of how they relate to Holden and to their own age group.

A 11 Reading chapters 21–26

In the third part of the novel, Holden meets with Mr Antolini and Phoebe, the two people he values most. Both meetings take a surprising turn: Holden is so deeply disappointed and shocked by Antolini's "flitty pass" that he "passes out." Holden seems to have reached an abyss. When Holden meets Phoebe after having lived through this crisis his relationship to Phoebe has changed. He no longer regards her as a kind of companion but as the child she in fact is. Now he is ready to take on a responsibility for her – and for his life too.

Sequence IV: Return home

A 12 "'Boy, do I hate it,' I said. 'But it isn't just that. It's everything.'" – Holden's escapism

Dissatisfied with his own personal life and the phoniness and complexity of the grown-up world, Holden develops four avenues of escape (The Museum of Natural History, pp. 108–110, Massachusetts/Vermont, pp. 118–121, "Out West/deaf mute," pp. 178–180, and "My cabin," p. 184). While the museum represents a confrontation with death and the ephemeral (nothing changes), the other three places are all situated in nature, far from human beings. The retreat to nature is a typically romantic motif as in Wordsworth's poem "Daffodils." This poem shows the same ambiguity towards nature as Holden in his escape from reality – the poet does not want a permanent retreat into nature, but he wants to be constantly in spiritual touch with his memories of the daffodils. A similar theme can be found in Henry Thoreau's "Walden." (Cf. *J. D. Salinger "The Catcher in the Rye." – Annotations and Study Aids* by Rudolph F. Rau, Stuttgart et al.: Klett 1999, Klettbuch 573808) Holden does not want total seclusion from human society – he envisages a family and some kind of outside job.

A 12

1. Questionnaire
Its aim is to induce students to think critically about their own personal situation and their relationship to the grown-up world. The 'reasons' should be compared to assignment no. 5, the 'qualities' with no. 6 in A 10. The category 'place' could be analyzed with respect to the dichotomy 'nature' vs. 'big city' and should be related to the area (village or rural area vs. city) where students come from.

2. Museum of Natural History (pp. 108–110)
A museum is a place where things from the past are kept. Holden likes the museum because the things there don't change any more – they are reliable. His love for the museum represents his longing for the kind of unequivocal orientation he lacks. The fact that he doesn't go into the museum after all can be seen as a sign that he is ready to face an uncertain future.

3. Massachusetts/Vermont (pp. 118–121)
The two photos help students to accomplish this assignment by stressing the difference between urban and rural life. Holden hates almost everything about New York.
Essential characteristics of life in Vermont: - natural beauty, manual work, seclusion, marriage.
The retreat from civilization to an unspoilt countryside is a central topic in literature, especially popular with the Romantic movement. Students may want to read and discuss Wordsworth's poem *Daffodils* and compare his experiences with Holden's.

4. "Out West/deaf mute" (pp. 178–180)
After the disastrous visit to Antolini Holden feels completely down. Sitting on a park bench (p. 178 f.) he phantasizes about an ideal relationship with a girl that works but implies as little communication as possible. The cartoon visualizes Holden's day dream.
The assignment gives students the possibility of experiencing herself/himself what such a 'utopia' might be like.
Main characteristics: *pretty landscape, sun, beautiful wife, no social intercourse, no conversations, a job, children (hidden from view).*
Paradox: *having a wife and children means having some sort of social relationship even if it is on a small scale.*

5. "My cabin" (p. 184) *(See diagram.)*
Holden feels that the grown-up world is full of phoniness and that all social relationships in the world of grown-ups are beyond his control. He therefore dreams of retreating from that world to his "cabin," where he can be in complete control. Only members of the family are to be admitted, especially Phoebe; even they must comply with his rules.

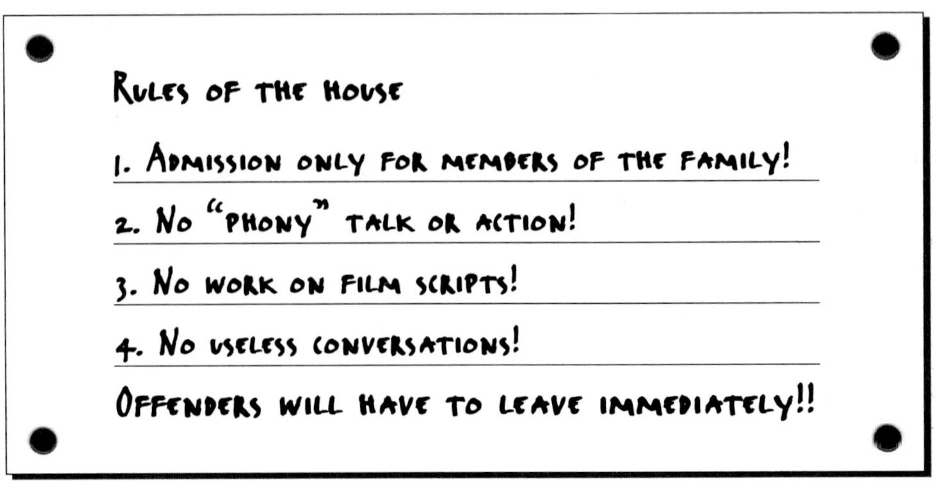

A 13 "Kids look all right" – Children and childhood

The following assignments focus on Holden's view of children and childhood. He's extremely fond of children partly because he sees them as totally innocent beings and partly because they don't belong to the adult world he himself can't cope with. When closely looked at his "catcher-dream" it sounds rather immature. Preventing children from growing up doesn't solve problems – it just mirrors Holden's own inability to come to terms with the adult world.

1. The loss of innocence

In this poem, Robert Frost formulates a universal "law of nature:" Everything "gold" is ordained to decay. If we replace "gold" with "innocence," Holden's assuming the role of "the catcher" appears as a hopeless attempt to defy the universal laws of nature.
The photo of the children playing may help students understand what Holden finds so attractive about childhood.

2. Children in the novel *(See table.)*

Allie (p. 33)	Singing boy (p. 104)	Phoebe (pp. 143–158)
left-handed with glaring red hair *very intelligent, interested in poetry* *great sense of humour* *the nicest in the family*	*walks parallel to the curb on the street* *does not mind the traffic* *sings joyfully*	*looks alright when sleeping (144)* *dances well (158)* *spontaneous and incalculable (149)* *creative, original in her thinking (144–145)* *always listening when you tell her something (150)*

All children are spontaneous, creative, and unconcerned about the rules of the adult world.

3. Phoebe's probing questions (pp. 152–156)

This analysis of Holden's conversation with Phoebe aims at showing how immature some of Holden's views are.

- *Holden likes the two nuns who have dedicated their lives to helping the needy and downtrodden; James Castle, who sticks to his opinion and as a result commits suicide; his dead brother Allie; his conversation with Phoebe; he would like to be "the catcher in the rye," who saves thousands of children from falling down the cliff.*
- *Holden is at odds with the whole grown-up world, Phoebe's probing questions force him to give expression to his ideals.*
- *Holden suspects that most lawyers only want to make money, not to save "innocent guys' lives." And even if you are idealistic, it's hard to determine what the motive is: if it's to save innocent people or to gain prestige.*
- *Phoebe quite realistically thinks that constantly concerning oneself with dead people or being together with a 12-year old girl, "just chewing the fat and horsing around" hardly provide any sensible perspective for a 17-year old boy.*

4. Holden's "catcher-dream" (pp. 155–156)

(See diagram below.)
What Holden's catcher-dream really means is that he wants to prevent children from growing-up and face the world as it is. The speaker in the text wants to help children to find their way in the grown-up world.

5. The "original"

Students may want to read the poem by Robert Burns.

world of children ←→	world of grown-ups
joyful *sincere* *imaginative* *innocent* *attentive*	*"phony"* *unimaginative* *"crumby"* *inattentive*

A 14 "Apply yourself!" – Antolini's advice

The following assignments focus on Holden's conversation with Mr Antolini in chapter 24. This conversation is an important turning-point in the novel. Though the meeting with Antolini ends disastrously the conversation, in fact, marks the beginning of Holden's development towards maturity.

1. Two pictures

The pictures can help students to again bring into focus Holden's confused state of mind. The left picture appears to be well ordered, the right picture quite chaotic. Holden would definitely prefer the right picture.

2. Becoming conscious of yourself or: Your "Antolini-level"

The test is devised in such a way that Holden would have scored 15 points.

Antolini's prognoses: *He might find level I perhaps as a bit too rational and warn of unforeseeable events; he might be most optimistic about level II. Level III might require more attention. In the case of level IV his prognosis would be the same as for Holden.*

The distribution of scores in class: The result is the class's "level of maturity."

In addition, it might be interesting to discuss individual questions/statements from the test within the whole class.

3. Being grown-up

Practically everything depends on whether students agree with Holden's rejection of the grown-up world, or whether they agree more with the idea of maturity as is generally accepted by grown-ups.

4. Holden's state of maturity

1. *Old Luce* 2. *Ackley* 3. *Mrs Hayes* 4. *Mr Spencer* 5. *Old Luce.*

5. A digression on "digressions"

Reading the excerpt from Sterne's "Tristram Shandy" will give the students a fairly good idea of what is meant by the term "digression" – a term that is central to the conversation between Holden and Mr Antolini (pp. 165 ff.). When discussing the text students can form their own opinion about the usefulness of digression in written works or discussions. In this way the next assignment can be prepared.

Probably students need some help with this kind of old-fashioned syntax. Therefore, it might be a good idea to have them first determine the main clauses and have them write a brief summary of the text. Then the students can be asked to find out the digressions.

a) Summary: *While my parents were making love, which led to my begetting, my mother asked my father whether he had wound up the clock. My father was shocked. Probably, I would have been another person, if this interruption had not happened.*

b) Digressions: *There are two long digressions, the first deals with the consequences of the sexual act with regard to the future off-spring, the second with the nature and importance of the sexual impulse.*

6. Antolini's advice

a) "Digression:" *Antolini seeks to find priorities ("there's a time and place for everything," p. 166) as a way of simplifying the complexities of life. Holden prefers to digress, – a reflection of his spontaneity, little emotional control.*

"Terrible fall:" *It happens to people whose aims are beyond being realistically achieved (cf. Holden's desire to be "the catcher") or those who don't bother because they see no possibility of their goals ever being achieved. In both cases, the result is complete frustration or dissatisfaction with life (cf. "The man falling isn't permitted to feel or hear himself hit bottom.", p. 169). One is then left with a feeling of jealousy, an education that is useless and superficial, or a mindless job.*

Stekel-quotation: *Mature men do not follow high-flown ideals which are "noble" to die for, but have realistic aims appropriate to the 'particular size of their minds.' – and they do this 'humbly.' (cf. p. 171). One of Holden's first aims should be to find realistic goals for himself ("you're going to have to find out where you want to go," p. 170) and to pursue them without hesitation.*

Education: *Education may help in the search for direction and identity; in books one can often find characters or persons who have similar problems ("you're not the first person who ...," p. 170) and possible solutions to these problems as well. Being educated people these authors are more likely to elucidate a problem or conflict with clarity and precision, and are perhaps more capable of finding the appropriate solution.*

b) + c) Refutation: *Antolini's philosophy is too rational and leaves out all emotions. Apart from that, he tends to underestimate the complexity of the real world.*

Antolini – Old Luce: *Both advise Holden to find out the "patterns of his mind" (cf. p. 133) but Old Luce seems to think conforming to the rules of society is more important ("he's helped me to adjust myself ...," p. 134) as Mr Spencer ("life is a game that one plays according to the rules," p. 7). On the other hand, Old Luce's reference to the East and his understanding of sex as a "physical and spiritual experience" (p. 132) seems more balanced than Antolini's one-sided rationalism.*

Antolini's philosophy ◄──►	**Refutation**
rationality	*emotions/imagination*
direction	*openness to experience*
education	*spontaneity*
pragmatism	*idealism*

7. Adolescents with a "direction in life"

The two authentic texts may help to make the questions easier to answer. *Gretchen is self-centered and is, in spite of her dreams of wealth and glamour, ready to live a humble ordinary middle-class life. She is a pragmatist.*

Eduardo is very purposeful, he has a "plan." In contrast to Gretchen, money's primary purpose is to enable him to write his great novel with a message. He shows much more commitment to and awareness about the world around him than Gretchen (although he's three years younger) and wants "to do something for the world." He is an idealist; like Holden; he dreams of saving children from the dangers of the world, but not on such a grand scale.

Cf. also "At 16, they control their lives" on p. 60.

8. The "flitty pass" (pp. 172–175)

The additional text on homosexuality may serve as a starting-point for a discussion on homosexuality although a discussion of this problem is not compulsory.

a) It does not matter whether Antolini is a homosexual or not. Of interest is only Holden's reaction to this incident.

b) Holden is completely appalled by the Antolini incident and wishes to flee this traumatic experience as quickly as he can. His frantic reaction might be the result of his latent fear of "crumby" sex (which for him probably includes homosexuality) and his constant search for human perfection.

c) Holden's remark: "I think I was more depressed than I ever was in my whole life." (p. 175) reflects the intensity of the shock. After a few of hours sleep, he begins to doubt whether his perception of the incident was correct: ("maybe I was wrong about thinking he was making a flitty pass at me," p. 175) and whether his judgement of Antolini wasn't a bit too hasty: "... even if he was a flit he certainly'd been very nice to me" (p. 175). Antolini, someone who could have given Holden spiritual guidance, turns out to be a deep disappointment. The result is even more confusion and deeper depression. Yet, this scene also contains the first sign of an eventual recovery from depression. For it is here that Holden comes close to accepting the imperfection of man. It is interesting to note that Holden who usually loses everything in his absent-mindedness is careful to save the paper with the Stekel quotation.

A 15 "I felt so damn happy all of a sudden" – Holden's crisis and change

The assignments deal with Holden's final crisis and change in chapters 25 and 26.

1. Holden's emotional development in chapter 25

This assignment may help students to find out the general structure of this pivotal chapter.
(See diagram next page.)

A 15

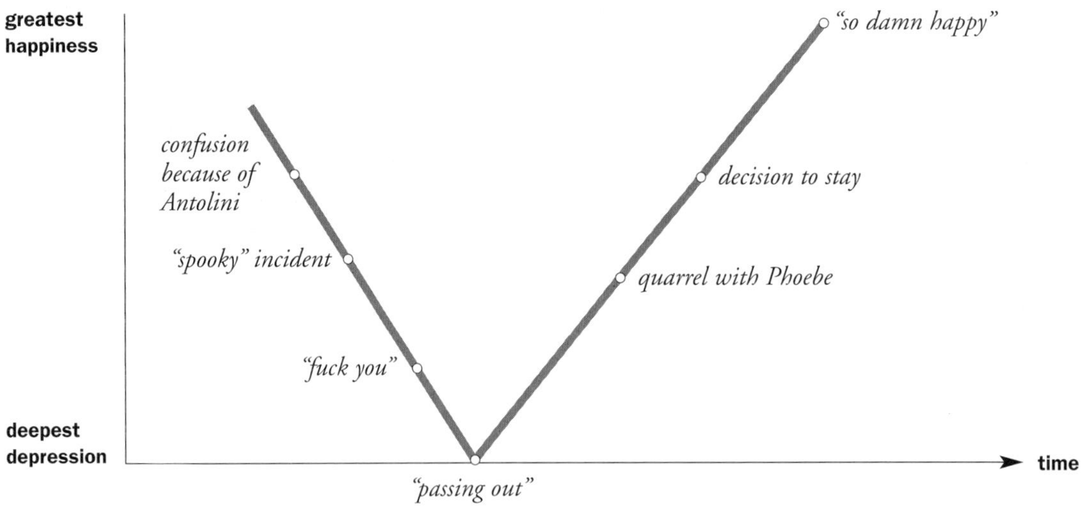

2. Holden's symbolic death and rebirth (pp. 175–184)

There is no simple one to one correlation between Holden's biography and the "rites of initiation" delineated in the additional text:

- Abduction: *Holden is not abducted but separates himself from his former environment by leaving Pencey Prep.*
- Loss of name: *Holden is not sure of his identity and therefore uses false names (cf. A 10).*
- Wounded and devoured by monster: *The "monster" in Holden's case is the grown-up world with all its phoniness and imperfection that makes him "pass out." The symbolism of this "death" is given an additional dimension by its occurring in a museum that exhibits mummies.*
- Purification by symbolic cleansing: *Holden faints in a public toilet.*
- Symbolic rebirth and new identity: *Holden feels responsible for Phoebe.*

3. Holden's change

Sally represents the values of the grown-up world, and it is she who quarrels with Holden because of his childish suggestion to elope. In the quarrel with Phoebe, Holden at first wishes to escape to the West without considering the consequences. He then begins to assume the responsibilities of a mature adult when he decides to stay and care for his sister. Another sign of Holden's increasing maturity is the comment: "If they fall off, they fall off" (p. 190).

He no longer wants to be "the catcher." Children should be able to develop without outside interference even at the risk of their failing completely.

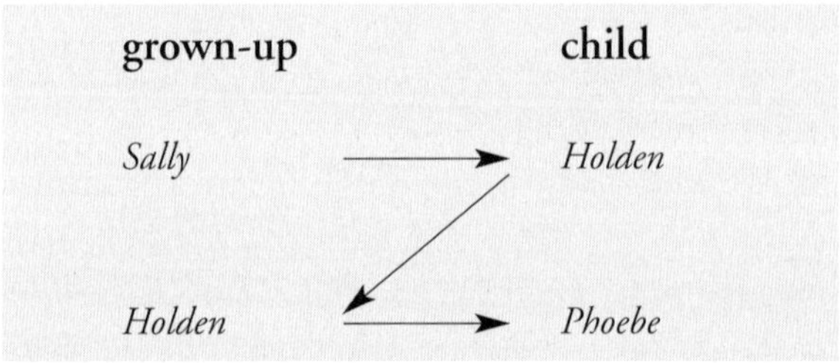

4. The red hunting hat

The symbolic meaning of the red hunting hat includes all the four alternatives that are presented here. The quotation here shows the hat is no longer of any use to Holden – it "got soaked anyway" (p. 191) – and is passed on to Phoebe, who is soon going to have to find her own way of achieving maturity.

5. Holden's past, present, and future

Past:

- *His conversation with Antolini (= gives him crucial advice)*
- *His decision to stay (= general acceptance of society)*
- *His sending Phoebe back to school (= acceptance of responsibility)*
- *The renunciation of his role as "the catcher" (= acceptance of the world as it is)*

Present:

a) *Antolini has tried to show Holden that the literary tradition can provide meaning and direction to one's own personal life. Holden's present attempt to write down his recent experiences is proof that he, at least partially, has understood Antolini's advice. But Holden still*

A 15

doesn't have the intellectual prowess or maturity to properly evaluate his experiences and adventures.

b) "I don't know what I think about it," (p. 192). This observation about Holden is given further confirmation when considering Holden's chaotic manner of narration and his many digressions (cf. the discussion about digression in chapter 24). Unlike Antolini, Holden offers no advice as to how to deal with problems similar to his own. It is left to the reader to sift through Holden's disjointed narrative and to draw his or her own conclusions.

Future:

a) Holden has not completely changed. He is still unable to establish rational guidelines for his own future ("how do you know what you're going to do till you do it," p. 192). He is obviously still too ambivalent about how to deal with the future; he does not show the determination that Antolini might have expected.
The novel ends with Holden's very noble gesture of general forgiveness ("I even miss that goddam Maurice"), thus showing that he is willing to accept the imperfection of man.

b) Holden's future remains uncertain, because he has still not found out "where he wants to go" (cf. p. 170).

The diagram depicting Holden's various emotional states as they are revealed in the novel could look as the following:

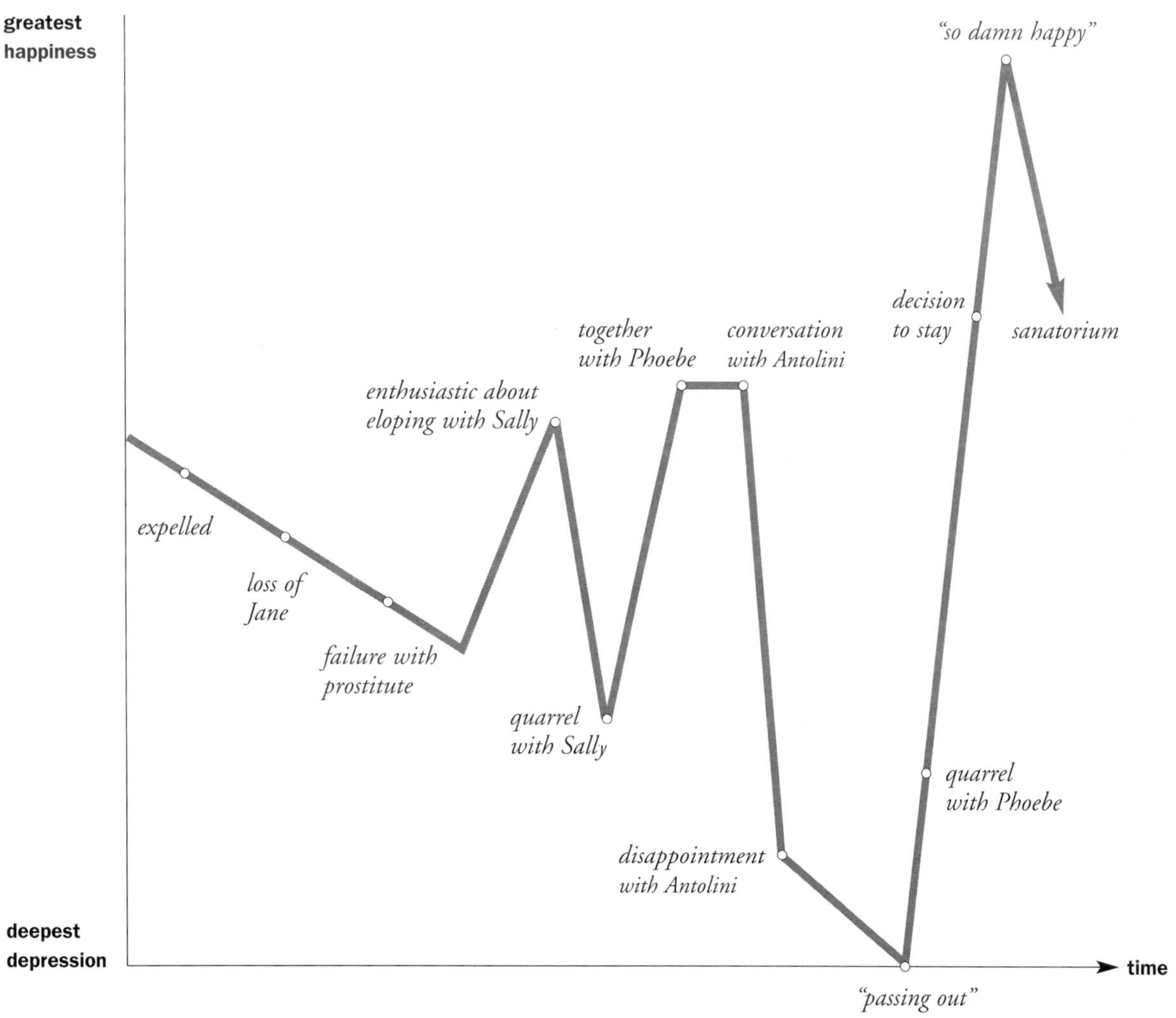

After rising to the heights of exuberance and exhilaration at the end of chapter 25, Holden returns to a more normal state of mind in chapter 26. The latter state of mind is by no means completely bad if we consider that Holden was depressed most of the time. Here normal now means that Holden is not out West but in a sanatorium that is sanctioned by a "phony" society. We can assume that at the moment of Holden's breakdown he was not willingly a patient at the sanatorium, but later resigned himself to the need for a long period of psychoanalytical treatment. His acceptance of this treatment could possibly signify that Holden is ready to accept the norms of society. (cf. p. 154). It is conceivable to think that Holden's decision not to go West with Phoebe anticipates his making peace with society. It is up to the reader to decide if this denouement is deplorable, a sign of weakness, or a laudable sign of maturity.

6. Topics for discussion

a) *It is difficult to draw any definite conclusions about the open ending of the novel. Much depends on the individual reader's view of grown-ups and what society should be like. We could decide that the novel is optimistic: Holden will be able to cope with his problems and somehow find his place in society. Or we could decide that the novel is pessimistic: Holden will never be able to cope with a "phony society" even after his release from the sanatorium.*
If we consider the author's own life and his attempt to escape from society (cf. A 17), we might tend to think that the novel is more pessimistic in nature.

b) *Hamilton's statement causes us to wonder about youth rebellion in general and Holden's rebellion in particular. We certainly can accept Holden's criticism of the adult world. Hamilton's assertion that Holden is a complete nihilist (he … "is not for anything …") is an oversimplification, though we should note that Phoebe criticizes her brother: "You don't love anything." Should Holden have gone completely mad or gone through with one of his foolhardy schemes to show himself to be a true rebel? It is indeed paradoxical that Holden himself is a phony because he cannot live up the ideals he espouses for others.*

A 16 "The Catcher in the Rye" – General discussion

1. Kind of novel

The text from the Encyclopaedia Britannica can be given to a student, who should research the plots of the novels under consideration in a source book about literature and report his/her results to the class.
There are definitely elements of the "Bildungsroman" in the novel, but there is social criticism as well. Holden's criticism of the phoniness of the adult world is valid even if it means compromising oneself in order to survive in such a society, and this need to compromise in an imperfect world is the moral lesson of the novel.

2. Contemporary reception of "The Catcher in the Rye"

Text A (from a well-known religious newspaper in America):

- *Positive: skillfully written, quick-moving story*
- *Negative: foul language; not fit for children in spite of the author's assertion; repellent mixture of vulgarity, naïveté, and sly perversion; Holden is a kind of hypersensitive psychopath, whose "tale" might persuade young readers to imitate him ("may multiply his kind").*

In summary the novel is seen to be nothing more than a story about a rather unbalanced young man. For this reason the book has been banned in some American schools to this very day.

Text B:

In this review, the novel is praised for the authenticity of its language and the way Holden's emotions and experiences are depicted. Holden is seen as a boy who craves for understanding and affection in an otherwise phony world. The novel is attested a "wry humour" and for the creation of one of the most charming and delightful child figures in modern fiction. Not all readers would agree that Holden's experiences were "horrifying," or that Antolini's advice to Holden was useless.

3. A look at what's in the Internet
The first letter reveals a deep emotional response to the novel, whereas the second one seems to doubt whether Holden is representative of today's youth. This would be an opportune time to deal with assignment 4.
Students should be warned that the English found on the Internet may not always be correct.
Hopefully students will be motivated to write their own "letter to Mr Salinger" after having visited this website, even if they didn't like the novel.

4. Relevance of "The Catcher in the Rye"
Students are expected to draw conclusions about the relevance of the novel to their own lives and experiences. A profound knowledge of literary history cannot be presumed at this level.

5. The results and uses of literary analysis
These questions are meant to permit an evaluation of your teaching and to determine how successfully the skills of literary analysis as prescribed by the curriculum were learned. The comments made by the students should be taken seriously.

A 17 "Refusal to communicate" – J. D. Salinger

The biography of an author is often not pertinent to an understanding of his/her work. In the case of Salinger, the novel and his life are inextricably bound with each other: While the fictional hero finally comes to accept society as it is. Salinger has, on the other hand, decided to lead the life of a hermit, isolated from the rest of society just with his wife on a farm in New Hampshire, a farm that is reminiscent of Holden's "cabin" in New England. Salinger has been unable to come to terms with society, unlike the hero he created himself. "Catcher in the Rye" did not function as a therapy for the author, although it is said that literature often has this function. We need only think of Werther's suicide preventing Goethe from doing the same himself.

1. Parallels between Salinger's life and "The Catcher in the Rye"
The parallel is obvious – he did what his hero Holden couldn't do in the novel. After the success of "Catcher in the Rye" in 1953 he retreated to a "cabin" in New Hampshire and broke off most contacts with the rest of the world, especially with journalists. Salinger may have communicated in some way with his wives, but we wonder if it wasn't a bit the way Holden described his vision of life in a cabin: nothing spoken, everything written on paper. It is interesting to note that his first wife divorced him because of "indifference and refusal to communicate." In 1971, the only interview he had given since 1953, and indeed the last interview given to this date, he explained why he didn't want to publish anything any more: "There is a marvelous peace in not publishing. It's peaceful. Still, publishing is a terrible invasion of my privacy. I like to write. I love to write. But I write just for myself and my own pleasure." This, of course, is a smack into Antolini's face who lectured Holden on the advantages of publishing.

2. The problem of privacy for celebrities
Students could discuss the many times celebrities are plagued by "papparazzis." It might be interesting to distinguish between celebrities in the entertainment industry, politics, sports, and the world of literature. How can those who appear on TV or on the screen expect more privacy than a writer?

3. Fictive interview
There should be a light-hearted approach to this interview. Anything is possible!

Additional materials: Problems of teenagers today

This collection of additional materials may be helpful if you want to deal with the situation and problems of today's teenagers more thoroughly.

How well do parents know their kids? (pp. 55–56)
This text points out that "loneliness" is the biggest problem for American teenagers and suggests that parents spend more time with their children and be more susceptible to their problems. Cf. also p. 63: "The secret life of teens."

Three statements on "fashion," "media violence," and "cliques" (p. 57)
These statements can serve as impulses for discussions about these problems.

A teenager's plea to parents (p. 57)
This text offers advice for parents how to deal with their teenagers, what they should "do" and what they should not do ("don't"). Before presenting this text, the students should try for themselves.

Teens by the numbers (pp. 58–59)
A collection of statistics referring to many aspects of the situation and behaviour of teenagers in the USA.

At 16, they control their lives. (p. 60)
Three examples of teenagers "with a direction in life." Cf. A 14, 7. Adolescents with a "direction in life."

Teenage girls. They really are worried sick (pp. 61–62)
The typical worries of English teenagers and what could be done against them. The article refers to problems with weight, health, bullying, smoking, drinking, drugs, school, money, and fitness. Do German teenagers have the same problems? Cf. also the authentic statements of American teenagers on pp. 64–68.

The secret life of teens (p. 63)
This article discusses the consequences of new technologies for the life of teenagers. The author maintains that the new technologies open for teens almost a "virtual reality without adults" which could lead to a further estrangement between teens and their parents.

Authentic statements (p. 64–68)
These statements of American teenagers refer to the following problems: Peer pressure, self-esteem, weight, cultural identity and racial problems.

Survey of contents

	Pages
Phoney conversation during the intermission (pp. 114 f.) With Sally in the ice palace (pp. 116–121) Quarrel with Sally about Holden's escapist phantasies (Massachusetts/Vermont) (pp. 118–121)	
Chapter 18: Stage show at Radio City Hall Girls, misjudging boys (pp. 122 f.) Making an appointment with Old Luce (p. 123) Stage show/the kettle drummer (pp. 123 f.) The phoney mother (p. 126) Brother D.B. on war (p. 126 f.)	122–127
Chapter 19: With Old Luce in the Wicker Bar The phonies in the Wicker Bar (p. 128) Old Luce (pp. 129 f.) Dialogue with Old Luce on sex and psychoanalysis (pp. 130–134)	128–134
Chapter 20: Holden being drunk Holden gets drunk (p. 135) Phone call to Sally (p. 136) Conversation with wardrobe girl (p. 138) Holden in Central Park: Phoebe's record breaks, Holden thinks of his burial, of Phoebe and Allie (pp. 138–141) Decision to go home (p. 141)	135–141

III. Return home

Chapter 21: At home with Phoebe (I) On Phoebe (pp. 143–145) Dialogue with Phoebe on her latest experiences (pp. 146–149) Holden thinks about going to Colorado (p. 149)	142–149
Chapter 22: At home with Phoebe (II) Reasons for Holden's failure at school (pp. 150–152) What Holden likes: the two nuns, James Castle (pp. 153 f.) Holden's ideas on jobs: his catcher-dream (pp. 155 f.)	150–156
Chapter 23: Holden leaving home On Mr Antolini (p. 157) Dance with Phoebe (pp. 157 f.) Dialogue between mother and Phoebe (pp. 159 f.) Taking leave from Phoebe (pp. 161 f.)	157–162
Chapter 24: At Mr Antolini's On the Antolinis (p. 163) Antolini's "lecture:" digression (p. 166), terrible fall (p. 168), Stekel quotation (p. 169), the benefits of education (pp. 170 f.)	163–174

WEITERE TITEL

ENGLISCH

SEKUNDARSTUFE I

Arbeitsblätter **Englische Grammatik 5./6. Schuljahr**
43 Arbeitsblätter für einen kommunikativen Grammatikunterricht
ISBN 3-12-927874-5

Arbeitsblätter **Englische Grammatik 7./8. Schuljahr**
34 Arbeitsblätter für einen kommunikativen Grammatikunterricht
ISBN 3-12-927875-3

Arbeitsblätter **Englische Grammatik 9./10. Schuljahr**
32 Arbeitsblätter für einen kommunikativen Grammatikunterricht
ISBN 3-12-927884-2

Arbeitsblätter **Vertretungsstunden Englisch in der Sekundarstufe I**
60 Arbeitsblätter mit Lösungsangaben
ISBN 3-12-927895-8

Arbeitsblätter **Oskar Wilde: The Canterville Ghost/ Arthur Conan Doyle: The Speckled Band**
Zwei Lektüreeinheiten für die Klassen 6/7
40 Arbeitsblätter mit didaktisch-methodischen Kommentaren
ISBN 3-12-927885-0

SEKUNDARSTUFE II

Arbeitsblätter **Willy Russel "Educating Rita"**
19 Arbeitsblätter für einen handlungs- und produktionsorientierten Literaturunterricht
ISBN 3-12-927893-1

Arbeitsblätter **George Orwell "Animal Farm"**
22 Arbeitsblätter mit didaktisch-methodischen Kommentaren
ISBN 3-12-927899-0

Arbeitsblätter **G. B. Shaw "Pygmalion"**
16 Arbeitsblätter für einen handlungs- und produktionsorientierten Literaturunterricht
ISBN 3-12-927892-3

Arbeitsblätter **Barriers and bridges – intercultural conflicts and encounters**
18 Arbeitsblätter mit didaktisch-methodischen Kommentaren
ISBN 3-12-927902-4

Arbeitsblätter **The American dream – promise and reality**
30 Arbeitsblätter mit didaktisch-methodischen Kommentaren
ISBN 3-12-927804-4

Arbeitsblätter **J. D. Salinger "Catcher in the Rye"**
17 Arbeitsblätter mit didaktisch-methodischen Kommentaren
ISBN 3-12-927803-6

Unterrichtsideen
Textarbeit im Englischunterricht der Sekundarstufe II
ISBN 3-12-922694-X

Unterrichtsideen
Literatur im Englischunterricht der Sekundarstufe II
ISBN 3-12-922722-9

Notizen VOCAB

10R1 10R2

6.2. to nod
posture
dough
prep school
phony
qualms

7.2. to give a speech
deliver
guts - bowels
to hate sb's guts
to spill one's guts
gutsy
to have guts
impostor
phony
bury
coffin
undertaker

to mock sb.
house-owner
lasalord (- lady
to queue
~~to nod~~
~~posture~~
~~dough~~
EMOTIONS (11)
SCHOOL (p.12)

14.2.
an heir
to inherit
to be acquainted with
to be attached to
a branch
to create suspense

Notizen

Notizen